Irish Nineteenth Century Prison Records:

Survey and Evaluation

Denise M. Dowdall

HISTORYEYE
Dublin

Published by HISTORYEYE
94 Merrion Park ,
Blackrock,
County Dublin,
Ireland
www.historyeye.ie

FIRST EDITION

ISBN 978-0-9574021-4-0

Contents

Acknowledgements   *vi*

List of Illustrations   *vii*

Abbreviations   *vii*

Glossary   *viii*

Chronology   *x*

Introduction   *xiii*

1 *'Cease to do Evil. Learn to do Well'*
   The Richmond Bridewell..1

2 Castlebar: Study of a Travelling Community.....................3

3 *'The Cranmore Hotel'* : Sligo County Jail 13

4 *Under the Influence*
   The Ennis Inebriate Reformatory..............................18

5 *'Conducive to greater propriety of conduct'*
   Grangegorman Lane Women's Prison............................21

6 *'Eager to draw attention to everything he considered a defect'* : Tralee Jail...................................27

7 Kilmainham : A Century of Penal History.........................32

8 *'The Most perfect institution of its kind in Ireland'* Cork County Jail..37

9 *'The Women's Jail'* : Cork City Jail...........................39

10 *'The person is for ever released, but the property never....'* Debtors' Records..41

11 *'A Sad Evil'* : Newgate Gaol..................................48

12 *'Under a Novel Principle'* : Mountjoy Jail.....................51

13 Prisons of Strangers: Naas and Athy...........................53

14 *'The Iron Jail'* : Philipstown Government Prison..............59

15 The Criminalizing of Lunatics.................................62

16 *'The Most Disturbed District'* : Two Jails of Tipperary.......64

17 Complementary Records...68

18 The Challenge of Aliases......................................75

19 Conclusion...77

20 Appendix 1 : List of Available Jail Registers.................84

21 Appendix 2: List of Indexed Jail Registers 107

23 Appendix 3: List of Bridewells.....................................113

24 Appendix 4:.. 114
(a) List of Types of Prisons
(b) Jails examined for this project
(c) Types of Prison Record

25 Appendix 5: List of Debtors in Kilmainham Jail,
    1845-1867 116

Bibliography..*155*

Index *163*

ACKNOWLEDGEMENTS

This book arose out of an initial project undertaken in fulfillment of a Diploma in Genealogy at the National University of Ireland, Dublin. I would like to thank my tutor for this course, Sean J. Murphy MA, for his guidance and advice on the historical themes of this book. I would also like to give a word of gratitude to the archivists and staff at the National Archives, Bishop's Street Dublin, for their input and suggestions during my research . Many thanks too to the staff of the James Joyce Library at University College Dublin and of the National Library Dublin.

LIST OF ILLUSTRATIONS

(i) Entrance to St Michan's Park , Dublin, showing the outline of the old turreted corner of Newgate Gaol.
(ii) Facade of Grangegorman Lane Women's Prison, Grangegorman, Dublin
(iii) Main entrance of Richmond Bridewell Prison, South Circular Road, Dublin

ABBREVIATIONS

CPB- Convict Prison Board (Established 1854-5)
CRB - Convict Reference Books
CRF - Convict Reference Files
ESRI - Economic and Social Research Institute
GPO -General Prisons Office
GPB- General Prison Board (1877-8)
GRO - General Record Office
HCPP - House of Commons Parliamentary Papers.
HMPS - Her/His Majesty's Prison Service.
MFGS -Microfilm of the Genealogical Society of Utah.
MFS- Microfilm Security.
NA - National Archives, Bishop Street, Dublin.
NLI - National Library of Ireland, Kildare Street,Dublin.
PRONI - Public Record Office of Northern Ireland, Belfast.
ROD - Registry of Deeds, King's Inn, Dublin.
SIPD- Society for the Improvement of Prison Discipline.

GLOSSARY

Assizes. 19th century version of Circuit Court. Jury tried. Held in Spring and Summer. Dealt with the most serious offences submitted by the Quarter Sessions.

Bridewell. A detention centre for prisoners who have not yet been tried or whose sentence does not exceed seven days. Usually located near a courthouse or police station. Prisoner records usually not as detailed.

Convict. Person convicted to either death or transportation. From 1853 onwards the term denoted a person sentenced to a long sentence of penal servitude in the state.

Convict Depot. Examples Spike Island, Fort Carlisle. Unique to Ireland, these places which were often old forts, were used to house convicts, sometimes for quite long periods, prior to embarkation up to the early 1850s, or transfer to a convict prison thereafter.

Crofton System. A three-stage system in government prisons designed to incentivize a convict to return to society under supervision. Prisoner was graded each month under three headings - Discipline, (D)Schooling(S), and Industry(I). Points built up on that basis.

Grand Jury . System of local government in 19th century dating back to Norman times in which local land owners, appointed by a high sheriff, were charged with organizing the building, maintenance and administration of county jails among other institutions.

Habeus Corpus . Concept protecting right of a prisoner in which a custodian must have authority to detain a prisoner or else release him. Suspended during times of turbulence such as the Fenian uprising.

Intermediate Prison. Example Lusk, County Dublin. Under the Crofton Reform System, a jail where male prisoners were sent after successful completion of penal servitude to prepare them for the outside world. Emphasis on trade learning or agricultural work. Female convicts didn't enjoy the benefit of intermediate prisons, but served out their full sentence at the penitentiary before release, usually to a refuge.

Juvenile offender. Prison inmate under the age of fifteen. Sixteen and under from 1855.

Penitentiary. e.g. Richmond Penitentiary Grangegorman, opened in 1821. Embodied the principles of prison reformers like Jeremy Bentham that prisons should be places of personal rehabilitation and reflection.

Petty Sessions. Like a district court. Dealt with minor offences. Non jury. Local . Presided over by a magistrate. Extensive records available in the National Archives. Less detailed than prison registers, however, giving no physical description or prisoner address and seldom an occupation. Copies often copied in negative form.

Quarter Sessions. Held four times a year usually in county towns for more serious offences.

CHRONOLOGY

1780-1: Newgate Jail opens at Green Street, Dublin, replacing an old jail at Thomas Street.

1777: Prison reformer, John Howard, publishes the influential *The State of Prisons in England and Wales,* which provides impetus for penal reform that exists to this day.

1786: Inspector General of Prisons established to visit prisons once a year to ensure standards.

1788: Legislation passed by the House of Commons regularizing the running and construction of jails. Thirty three jail projects begun in Ireland.

1792: Irish Hard Labour Act passed.

1797: New Kilmainham Jail opened as the county jail for Dublin.

1812: Tralee Jail opens.

1816 : Royal Irish Constabulary founded, replacing a less formal force reliant on local yeomanry and militia forces.

1819: Society for Improvement of Prison Discipline (SIPD) founded to lobby for prison reform. Quakers like Elizabeth Fry agitate for religious and educational instruction, and productive work for inmates, arguing they are the best route to reform.

1820s: Jails built at Tullamore, Kildare, Trim, Maryboro, Carlow, Mullingar, Galway,Cork.

1831: Specially designated jail for female offenders opens at Grangegorman Lane Dublin.

1833: Richmond Bridewell opens in Dublin. From 1837, it caters for all male prisoners, tried and untried.

1835: Penal Act passed. Principles of Solitary Confinement and Hard Labour reinforced.

1840: Separate Confinement Act enacted requiring separate cells for prisoners. Pentonville Prison opened. Transportation to New South Wales abolished.

1843: Daniel McNaughton murders Robert Peel's secretary in London. Acquitted on the grounds of insanity. Law changed to accommodate the concept of "Guilty but insane" verdicts for first time.

1847-8: Prison system inundated due to the Famine.

1848: Transportation to Van Diemen's Land resumed if convict served portion of sentence in a penitentiary.

1849: Vagrancy Act passed . Large numbers of the population come into the prison system. Philipstown Jail reopened as a convict depot.

1850: Mountjoy opened to cater for convicts earmarked for transportation. Dundrum Asylum opened for the criminally insane.

1853: Transportation to Antipodes ended. Penal servitude introduced.

1854: Walter Crofton and two other officials appointed to administer the Convict Prison Board (CPB).

1855: First report of the CPB issued. Far-reaching reforms undertaken. Improvement in county jail records noted after this date.

1858: Reform schools opened for juvenile prisoners, cutting time spent in regular jails to a minimum. Female convicts admitted to Mountjoy Jail.

1859: Athy Jail closed.

1863: Newgate Jail Dublin closes.

1864: Automatic jailing of debtors abolished. (Small Debtors Discharge Act 1864.)

1867: Dangerous Lunatics Act amended to end practice of committing lunatics to jail in order to access a county asylum.

1869: Habitual Offender Act passed. (See Grangegorman records.) Better registration and post-sentence supervision of criminals follows.

1871 : Legal provision made for photography of prisoners to be used and for the registers to be changed to include any particulars deemed suitable by the Lord Lieutenant from time to time.

1874: Four Courts Marshalsea for Debtors closes.

1877: General Prison's Board founded to centralize and regularize the prison system. Noticeable improvement in level of detail of county jail records after this date. A complete alphabetical register of Habitual Offenders begun.

1877-78: Increase in prison numbers noted for the first time in twenty-seven years, although the overall trend was downwards. Lord Lieutenant given power to transfer prisoners from one prison to another as space becomes available. (40 & 41 Vic., C49, S.37). Subsequent years see the transfer of large numbers of convicts to county jails. Photography used increasingly to record habitual criminals and convicts.

1879: Maryborough (Portlaoise) Jail designated a government prison for invalid male convicts. Eleven county jails downgraded to bridewells and fifty-two bridewells closed down completely, leaving forty-three in the country.

1882: GPB publishes its *Register of Habitual Criminals* containing over eight thousand names.

1887: Richmond Bridewell closes.

1897: Grangegorman Women's Prison closes.

1910: Kilmainham Jail closes.

Introduction

This project set out to assess the value of Irish prison records from the Nineteenth Century for genealogists and students of Irish history. While not over-looking convict records entirely, the project dealt mainly with the archives of county and city jails. The reason for this was numerical. In 1853, the year trans-portation from Ireland to the Antipodes officially ended, there were an estimated 3,764 male and 514 female convicts in Ireland.[1] This compared with a general prison population of 83,805 for the same year. [2] In 2012, major developments in record digitization made Irish prison records accessible on the internet for the first time,[3] opening up their secrets. This book is a response to this new accessibility and can perhaps serve as an accompaniment to the digitized records.

At all times the questions were asked - to what extent did the prison popu-lation represent the population at large and which crimes were the most familial? What kinds of information could be found out about these prisoners and the soci-ety that they lived in? What various uses could this information be put to?

Available records were examined for their state of preservation, legibility, standard, depth and scope in terms of population numbers and detail. Years cov-ered, chronological continuity and finding aids such as the presence of alphabeti-cal name indexes were noted. Extensive use was made of the yearly Inspector-General of Prisons Reports prepared for the House of Commons since 1822, as they were the best source of background information on the state of every prison

---

[1] http://myhome.ispdr.net.au/~mgrogan/cork/barracks.htm. Accessed 9th may 2010. Submitted by Michael Cronin.

[2] *Proquest Information and learning Centre,* 2005..House of Commons Parliamentary Papers On-line. 2006. http://parlipapers.chadwyck.co.uk 1854 [1803] Thirty-second report of the inspectors-general on the general state of the prisons of Ireland, 1853. Page 5. Accessed April 4 2011 via UCD Connect website.

[3] familysearch.org, accessed July 2013.

in the country and they helped to chart the course of penal reform in Nineteenth Century Ireland.

Prison registers come under the auspices of the Department of Justice which succeeded the Victorian General Prisons Board, founded in 1877. With the exception of the Philipstown Convict Depot records (1849- 1862) the original registers, which are located at the National Archives, Bishop Street, were microfilmed by members of the Church of Latter Day Saints in 2004, making them accessible on a self-service basis to the local researcher. There are forty-five prisons featured in this collection, taking up one hundred and sixty-three reels of microfilm. These records have subsequently become searchable by prisoner name on the *Familysearch* website.[4] They can be viewed in full at certain participating institutions and on some commercial websites for a fee. [5]

Most counties are represented in this archive but there are no surviving records for Donegal, Cavan, Monaghan, Westmeath, Roscommon or Louth . Northern Ireland's prison archives are available at the Public Record Office of Northern Ireland under the HMP collection. But with a typical starting date of 1870, they are far less historic than those at the Dublin National Archives. Cork is the county with the largest collection of surviving records (fourteen prisons), though a disproportionate number are bridewells, where prisoner details were inferior. (Appendix 3).

The oldest archive belongs to Kilmainham Jail with a starting date of 1797. This is the exception however. Numerous prison projects were undertaken in the early 1830s in response to greater crime levels caused, among other factors, by agrarian unrest accompanying the change from tillage to pasture. Prisons at Tullamore, Kildare, Trim, Portlaoise, Carlow, Nenagh ,Mullingar, and Galway date from this period, incorporating a radial building design to reflect new theories on prisoner supervision and classification.[6] In terms of surviving archives, only ten prisons cover the 1830s or before, while eleven prison archives begin in the 1840s. Official reports reveal that the registers were generally written up by a clerk specially hired for the job, hence the quality and uniformity of the handwriting. The clerk was usually aided in his work by an experienced prison officer, par-

---

[4] Ibid.

[5] www.findmypast.ie, accessed July 2013.

[6] Tim Carey. *Mountjoy - the Story of a Prison*. Page 32. Collins press, Wilton Cork. 2000.

ticularly when setting out references to a prisoner's former convictions. [7] The collection in the National Archives contains examples of many different types of registers, all with slightly different emphases and reflecting an acknowledgement of the importance of prisoner classification from very early on. Although it is highly likely that most jails kept a representative number of these registers, (Appendix 4), their survival rate has been poor. Consequently the General Register is the main stock of the archive.

Studies on a selection of prisons are presented below, chosen for their variety and points of interest. There is particular emphasis on Dublin prisons as Dublin is poorly served by the major Irish census substitutes of the Nineteenth Century.

[7] *Proquest.* House of Commons Parliamentary Papers Online. http://parlipapers.chadwyck.co.uk. 1847-48 [952] Prisons of Ireland. Twenty-sixth report of the Inspectors-General on the general state of the prisons of Ireland, 1847; with appendices. Accessed Mar 1 2011 . Subscription required.

'Cease to do Evil. Learn to do Well'
The Richmond Bridewell

Since 1837, Dublin's Richmond Bridewell on the South Circular Road was the city jail for all convicted male offenders, including juveniles. Consequently there are no women to be found in its registers apart from those found in a single book of female felons dating from 1830 to 1836 [8]. 'The Bridewell' had 314 cells under the penitentiary model of separating inmates day and night . The motto over the main door, *'Cease to do Evil. Learn to do Well'* summed up something of the penitentiary ethos, but in fact it had its origins in the jail's original use as a "House of Correction" for all vagrants of the city . The foundation stone of this institution was laid in 1813 by the Duke of Richmond. [9] With the proposed winding down of Newgate Jail on the north side of Dublin in the 1840s , Richmond was earmarked for the detaining of untried prisoners also. But the inundation caused by the Famine held up these plans until well into the 1850s.

Richmond was notorious for its lax regime. Prison Inspector reports were very critical on this point , especially for the years 1842-3 . In 1844 Daniel O'Connell served a seven month sentence, albeit in some luxury, on a charge of conspiring against the State.[10] Perhaps the lowest point in the prison's history came with the escape of prominent Fenian, James Stephens, in 1866. This resulted

---

[8] National Archives, Dublin, Richmond Bridewell Register of female prisoners 1830- Dec 3 1836. MFGS 51/140.

[9] James Warburon, James Whitelaw, Robert Walsh, *History of the City of Dublin*, Volume 2,T. Cadell and W. Davies, London, 1818. Googlebooks.

[10] Patrick M. Geoghegan. *Liberator. The Life and Death of Daniel O'Connell 1830-1847*. page 183-185.

in the Viceroy's dismissal of the prison's governor, the experienced Dominic Marques, after 28 years of service. Richmond was closed for good in 1887 and converted into what became known as Wellington Barracks. Today it is a private third level college.

The surviving Richmond records are available over fourteen microfilms at the National Archives. They run from 1830 to 1887/8 , apart from the years 1837 to 1844 which are missing. Serious water damage occurred to the general registers of the early 1860s which made them unreadable and too fragile to microfilm.

Like many of the jails studied for this project, Richmond Bridewell possesses a unique set of records. One such is the **Registry of Military Prisoners** from 1855 - 1878. [11] (Entries for 1858 are missing). The vast majority in this register were men who deserted either from the army or the militia. There are 1406 men listed in this document. Particulars on the prisoner include name, age, height, education, religion, place of birth, regiment and trade. Date of committal and discharge were also given along with 'number of days dieted', presumably a reference to days of pay withheld. Many of the deserters were Scottish and English, though Dublin deserters usually had their street addresses provided. There were 139 desertions in 1855 but this number halved through subsequent years until 1878 when there was a sudden increase again to 132.

Another unique document is the **Registry of Drunkards** from Jan 1st 1861- Sep 5th 1873. This appears to be one of the few surviving records of its kind for male offenders, though official reports would suggest it was routine for large jails to keep a separate ledger for this class of prisoner. There are 11,535 men on this list. Information to be found about the offender included name, age, religion, education, place of birth, date of sentence or fine. (Sentence was usually twenty-four hours in lieu of a fine of 1/6 or 2/ 6.) No trade,occupation or present address was provided . There were several instances of two or three brothers appearing on these pages, making the document useful to genealogists.

---

[11] National Archives,Dublin, Richmond Bridewell. Register of military prisoners. MFGS 51/ 072.

Study of a Travelling Community
Castlebar Jail

The county jail for Mayo was located at Castlebar from 1834 until its clo-sure on October 26, 1919. The long-term governor was a Captain Disney who later lost his life at Omagh Jail from Typhoid fever. [12] Castlebar's surviving re-cords make up a small archive of two reels of microfilm in the National Archives. [13] They begin quite late - October 1878 - and run continuously to 1919. Entries are detailed, legible and with unusual attention paid to marks on person. There is no name index at any stage . The inclusion of body weight can also be enlighten-ing as many prisoners come out weighing more than when they went in.

An odd numbering system was evident in the Castlebar prison register. From 1882 the prison year was calculated from April to March. This system con-tinued until 1896 when the register began anew on January 1st . There is evidence that other jails adopted this practice in the early 1880s too but quickly abandoned it. (Kilmainham tried it briefly in 1881, Tralee in 1883.)

What is noteworthy about the Castlebar records is the frequency of prison-ers who were of no fixed abode. Although they made up only a small fraction of the overall prison population, the Travelling Community featured more promi-nently here than in any other jail researched, including Sligo. These individuals were invariably referred to as 'Tinkers' by fortuitously thorough prison clerks .

---

[12] *The British Medical Journal*, March 11, 1882, page 349.

[13] National Archives , Dublin,MFGS 51/003-004.

In light of this, a survey was done of the Traveller population of Castlebar prison from 1878 to 1898. The survey concerned itself with surname gathering and frequency, migration patterns and family relationships. One hundred and fourteen individuals were identified. The prison service's diligence in recording age, marks and scars was useful here as it helped to differentiate between the many people with the same first name. (Traveller communities have tended to stick rigidly to the traditional system of naming first child after paternal grandparent and so on, leading to a very high incidence of individuals with the same name. [14])

All the Travellers surveyed in Castlebar jail were Catholic. The oldest was John Moran (Mohan?) of Cappagh, Castlebar, born 1794. Eight percent bore small pox scars. Unlike the settled population, crimes committed among relatives tended to be among in-laws rather than blood relations. This was especially the case for mothers and daughters-in-law.

Twenty-seven surnames were identified in this survey. The predominant surname was Mc(Mac)Donagh. It was over four times more common than the next numerically strongest surname, Cawley. There is some evidence from the general records that McDonaghs , Sweeneys and Wards intermarried frequently. Several collaborative crimes involved these surnames. An example would be the 'uttering of base coin' - a popular offence of the period. The following table lists numerical frequency of each surname over the twenty years.

Table 1: **Traveller Surnames**
McDonagh 36
Cawley 8
Sweeney 5
Casey 5
Joyce 5
Noon/ Noone 5
Reilly 5
Ward 5
Mohan /Maughan/ Moughan) 5
Murtagh 4
Burke 3
Moffatt 3
Mongan 3

---

[14] Sharon Gmelch. *Tinkers and Travellers.* O'Brien Press 1975. Page 39.

Murray 3
Skiffington 3
Collins 2
Daly 2
Quinn 2
Stokes 2
Cassidy 1
Enright (Ainright) 1
Gallagher 1
Hynes 1
Kerrigan 1
McCawley 1
Moran? 1 (might be Mohan)
Power 1

In spite of their migratory life, all Travellers seemed to know precisely where they were born and there was remarkable consistency over the twenty years in recorded place of birth. 39% were recorded as being of no fixed abode at time of imprisonment, although this figure may have been higher as townships were often given as place of residence. Only one individual , Martin McDonagh (born 1874) could not specify his birth place. 15% of the population were still living where they had been born.

Table 2: Documented place of birth of Traveller prisoners, 1878-1898.

Location	Numbers	Location	Numbers
Castlebar	11	Boyle	3
Swinford	8	Frenchpark Roscommon	3
Sligo (McDo-nagh)	7	Kiltimagh (Ca-sey)	3

Location	Numbers	Location	Numbers
Roscommon Town	6	Birr (McDonagh)	2
Ballina	5	Caltra Galway	2
Strokestown	4	Galway Town	2
Westport (Noone)	4	Longford (Stokes/Quinn)	2
Claremorris (Sweeney)	4	Ballinasloe	2
Athlone	3	Dunmore, Galway	2
Bel-laghy(Skiffing-ton)	3	Tuam, Galway	2
Foxford	1	Ballyhaunis	1
Tobercurry	1		

Table 3 : Breakdown of Place of birth by County

Mayo (52)	47%
Roscommon (23)	21%
Galway (12)	11%
Sligo (10)	9%
Longford (5)	5%
Westmeath (3)	3%

Twelve Travellers were from Leinster. Drogheda, birth place of John Cawley, sticks out as the only east coast location. 101 Travellers were from Connaught. The distribution of birth locations describes approximately an eighty mile circle of migration with the McDonaghs having the widest range . At 47 % , Mayo birth places were perhaps lower than expected.

Physical descriptions reveal that tattoos were popular, especially among the McDonaghs. Traveller women appeared to be the only group of females in Nineteenth Century jails to bear them. The fashion was for blue spots, and occasionally an initial or a cross, tattooed usually about the left hand near the thumb

Data on educational standards revealed that 22% (15 out of 69)of the Traveller men could read and write. Most of these were born in the 1860s. 33% had some literacy skills. It is possible that these skills were picked up in prison. Literacy was rarer among the 45 females surveyed. Only one female could read and write and this individual , Catherine Murray (b 1859), was recorded as illiterate until 1890. 13% of women had some literacy skills however. A comparison with the wider population may be found by using percentages of illiteracy for Mayo for relevant census years. In 1881, for instance, 42% of males and 50 % of females could not read and write. [15]

Table 4: Names and Birth Dates of Travellers with Literacy Skills.

Male literacy: total surveyed 69.
Read &Write:
Martin McDonagh (b. 1858) Patrick Noone (b. 1859). Martin McDonagh (b. 1860). David Joyce (b. 1846). Martin Murray (b. 1864). Michael Casey (b. 1866). William Cassidy(b. 1865). Charles Daly (b. 1835). James Noone (b. 1860). Samuel Power (b. 1867). Martin McDonagh (b. 1860). Pat Reilly (b. 1875) John Collins (b. 1867) Thomas Joyce (b. 1869) John McDonagh (b. 1863).

Read:
John Murtagh (b. 1844).

[15] *Proquest*. House of Commons Parliamentary Papers Online. http://parlipapers.chadwyck.co.uk 1882 [C.3268] Census of Ireland, 1881. Part I. Vol. IV. Province of Connaught. Page 409. Accessed May 1st 2011. Institutional subscription required.

Alphabet:
Martin Hynes (b. 1859). John Moran (Mohan?) (b. 1794). John Cawley (b. 1823). Martin McDonagh (b. 1813).

Female literacy: total surveyed 45.
Read &Write : 1 Catherine Murray (b. 1859. Referred to as illiterate until 1890.)
Read: Bridget Casey (b. 1856) Ellen Joyce (b. 1869) and Catherine Murtagh (b. 1867).
Alphabet : Winifred Joyce (b. 1840) and Catherine Forde (b. 1819).

  The prison officials were careful to distinguish between 'tinkers' and 'dealers' , some of whom were also of no fixed abode. But did they intersect at any point? Surnames were noticeably different . Typical dealer names included Morrison, Lacey, Daly, Hastings and Bolingbroke. (The latter is an interesting English toponymic confined in Ireland almost entirely to Swinford, Mayo, and with faint royal echoes through Henry IV.) In other cases there were dealers with names now associated with Travellers : Collins, Forde, Ward and Sheridan. On one or two occasions there was complicity between the two groups in perpetrating petty crime. Otherwise there was little evidence linking them.

  Several surnames which seem to have died out among present-day Travellers were noticed in these records. One is Skiffington, (variation Skeffington), found mainly in Ulster and thought to be an English toponymic derived from Leicestershire. [16] The name is recorded in the Annals of the Four Masters for the year 1532 with the arrival of Henry VIII's Lord Deputy, Sir William Skeffington. [17]The surname here is represented by a family from Bellaghy, near Charlestown. What is surprising about this surname, apart from the fact that it is not of Irish origin, is its rarity. (Matheson recorded only eight GRO births for the whole country in 1890. [18])

---

[16] Patrick Hanks & Flavia Hodges. *Dictionary of Surnames.* Page 495. Oxford Univ. Press, 1996.

[17] John O'Donovan, *Annals of the Kingdom of Ireland by the Four Masters*, Vol V ,1501-1588. Page 1413.

[18] Sir Robert E. Matheson, *A Special Report on the Surnames of Ireland with notes as to Numerical strength etc.* Alex Thom & Co., Dublin. 1909. page 71.

Another unusual Traveller name in the survey, again not of Irish origin, was Moffatt (variations Mofat ,Moffett, Moffitt, Mefet, Muffett), represented by a couple from Kilmain, subsequently living near Cong. It is a name found mainly in Scotland and Northern Ireland, and is said to be derived from the Gaelic version of a place in Dumfries. [19] There are fourteen Moffats (and variations) listed in Griffith's *Valuation* for Mayo, primarily in Tirawley but also in Kilmain (where the Moffatt Travellers originated). Moffitts of Tirawley were also listed in the Tithe Applotment books. [20]

A feature of both families was their use of distinctive first names - 'Mark' for Skiffington, 'Peter' for Moffatt. These names were rarely used among the wider Travelling community and may provide clues to particular ancestral connections. 'Arthur' was also uniquely popular among the Sligo McDonaghs. 'Martin' was by far the most popular first name in the survey (1 in 3). This compares with only 1.3 % for the population at large for the 1901 Census, for instance. [21] There was a narrower selection of female first names with traditional stock predominating, apart perhaps from the disproportionate prominence of 'Winifred'. 'Mary' was the most popular female name (1 in 3).

Table 5: Traveller First Names in order of popularity.

Male		Female	
Martin	18	Mary	13
Patrick	11	Ann	7
John	11	Ellen	7
Thomas	9	Catherine	6
William	4	Margaret	5

---

[19] Patrick Hanks & Flavia Hodges. *Dictionary of Surnames.* Page 370. Oxford Univ. Press, 1996.

[20] National Library of Ireland, *An Index of Surnames of Householders in Griffith's Valuation and Tithe Applotment Books Co. Mayo.* NLI 1964.

[21] Census of Ireland 1901, http://www.census.nationalarchives.ie/pages/1901, Accessed June 3rd 2011. (Forenames only entered in search box.)

Male		Female	
Arthur (McDonagh)	3	Winifred	3
James	3	Bridget	3
David	2	Rose Ann	1
Michael	2		
Terence	1		
Mark (Skiffington)	1		
Bryan (Skiffington)	1		
Peter(Moffatt)	1		
Samuel (Power)	1		

The reason why the Skiffington and Moffatt names died out among modern Travellers is worthy of speculation. Was it due to lack of critical mass? Were they absorbed into the more dominant surname groups. Or did they marry within the settled population? The Skiffingtons in particular were well integrated among other Traveller families, as there is evidence from databases available on the Familysearch website that they intermarried with McDonaghs, Reillys and especially Noons. But they also seemed to have been resident in the one place , Bellaghy, for a long time, effectively becoming settled early on.

GRO marriage records confirm that in 1875 Patrick Moffatt married a non-Traveller, Mary Naughton, daughter of a Ballinrobe carpenter, Thomas Naughton. The couple's 1901 Census return had them living in Church Lane,Ballinrobe ,with their six daughters. Their dwelling was third class with a stable and piggery. [22] The same year their only surviving son, Peter, married Bridget McInerney, again the daughter of a non-traveller. In the case of the Moffats it is suggested that a

---

combination of marrying into the settled community and giving up the migratory life led to their disestablishment.

A more recent survey of Traveller surnames from 1981 indicates that the McDonaghs made up only 20.9 % of the population in the Western region , losing ground to the Wards (69.9 %), Sweeneys (67.5 %),Mongans (47.5 %) , Maughans (41.5%) and Collins (28.9%) . [23] While Collins was more commonly seen among the dealers, the name did not feature particularly prominently among the Travellers from 1878-98. The difference suggests that migration by these families into the area gathered apace in the Twentieth Century.

The familiarity gained with Traveller families from the Castlebar records allowed the study to be widened to the older Longford and Sligo jail records, taking in a previous generation or two in some cases. Longford Jail's records start in the 1850s, but they don't provide physical description or occupation, so they are unreliable if studied in isolation. [24] Sligo Jail is more detailed, adopting the term 'Tinker' from 1860 and providing data on education and physique. Sligo Jail has been particularly useful in advancing information on the origins of the Skiffingtons. [25]A Martin Skiffington (b 1816), from Rivertown Sligo, likely grandfather of the Skiffingtons mentioned in Castlebar, was convicted of assaulting Thomas Feenaughty in 1848. In a later entry he was said to go by the alias of Martin Feenaughty. (Feenaghty, a name closely linked with the Clanconway area of Galway and Roscommon, underwent extensive anglicization to Finnerty throughout the Nineteenth Century .[26]). A family link with Feenaughty is therefore suggested , possibly through marriage. Older Sligo sources such as the Census of Elphin,1749, lists a Thomas Skivinton and his wife, Protestant, Cottier, living in the parish of St. John's, Sligo Town. [27] Also, intriguingly a Mark Skifington was

---

[23] David B. Rottman, *The Population Structure and living Circumstances of Irish Travellers: Results from 1981 Census of Traveller Families*, ESRI, Paper No. 131, July 1986.

[24] National Archives , Dublin,Longford Jail General Register, Jul 9 1856- Dec 23 1868. MFGS 51/158.

[25] Ibid, Sligo Jail General Register, Oct 13 1837- Dec 23 1857. MFGS 51/094-5.

[26] Edward MacLysaght, *More Irish Families*. O'Gorman Ltd. 1960. page 108.

[27] *Origins. Census of Elphin* 1749, http://www.origins.net. Accessed Feb 12, 2011. Commercial site.

listed by Griffith's *Valuation* as leasing land at Tintagh, Boyle, not ten miles from Rivertown, Sligo, in 1858. [28]

The Sligo records also established that one Traveller surveyed, Samuel Power, had a grandfather named Edward Power, a Protestant bell hanger, born in 1814. Other Traveller names to crop up in Sligo included Clyne, Weir and Heaney. At the same time a family of Protestant Travellers from Sligo town was represented by William and Charles Wilson, born 1840 and 1844 respectively.

The Castlebar records revealed a great diversity of Traveller surnames in Mayo as recently as the mid-Nineteenth Century. They provided solid information on patterns of intermarriage, close family ties and migration. They also show that longevity was a surprising feature of some major Traveller families like the McDonaghs .

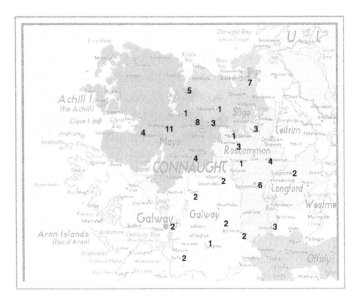

Map of Connaught showing Traveller prisoner birthplace and number of individuals involved. Birr ,Offaly ,(off the map) was the birthplace of two individuals.

[28] Ibid. Griffith's *Valuation*, http://www.origins.net. Accessed May 10, 2011.

'The Cranmore Hotel'
Sligo Jail

This prison, the jail for Sligo county, dates from 1823 and was closed in 1956. It was horse-shoe shaped with the governor's house located in the centre. It was nicknamed the 'Cranmore Hotel' by the locals, for whom gas heating and light were an exotic luxury.[29] Only half the original structure remains today, but at the time of printing of this guide there are ambitious plans by Sligo County Council, the present custodians , to preserve what's left of the jail as a living museum.[30]

A unique feature of this jail's surviving records is the substantial **Offences against Excise Register** running from 1836 to 1879. [31]Excise offenders were usually those engaged in the manufacture of illicit spirits, though tobacco manufacture was sometimes involved. There is some visible wear and tear in this book, reflected in the microfilm copy, but virtually all the entries were readable. Vital information on the offenders included name, age, date of committal, crime, sentence or fine and, from October 1838, religion. (Only 1 % of excise offenders were Protestant although they made up 9 % of the population for the county as late as 1861.[32]) There were a total of 1,307 names on this list. The usual sentence was three months in jail or a fine of £6. The average fine was increased to £20 in 1860. Part payment of fine and partial serving of sentence is a regular occurance, indicating that many offenders had some money. The activity must have been lucrative and worth the risk.

---

[29] *Sligo Jail*. http://www.sligotown.net/sligogaol.shtml. Accessed December 20 2010.

[30] Marese McDonagh, *Irish Times* . January 17, 2011.

[31] National Archives, Dublin,MFGS 51/094.

[32] *Proques*t,HCPP online, http://parlipapers.chadwyck.co.uk 1863 [3204-III] The census of Ireland for the year 1861. Part IV. Report and tables relating to the religious professions, education, and occupations of the people. Vol. II. Accessed June 4, 2011. Institutional Subscription required.

The townland location of an illegal still was often specified, particularly in the earlier decades of the list. For example - 'Bridget McDonagh(19) November 13th 1850, found in a mill at Castlebaldwin where malt was illegally grinding.' There was a great range of ages among the offenders. Both young and very old were included. Men and women in their eighties appeared, meaning they were born in the 1750s in the earlier pages. Prosecutions increased enormously in the Famine years, indicating that this marked the heyday of the illicit alcohol trade. There were 165 cases in 1848. This compares with only 62 cases in 1838 and a mere 9 cases in 1858.

The bringing in of several members of the same family was common and enhances the genealogical worth of this record. It highlights the domestic nature of these enterprises and the danger for anyone of even being found even within the vicinity of a still. At least 121 families were identified in this record. Repeat and even life-long offenders were commonly found, with inhabitants of Innismurray Island featuring prominently. Some case examples illustrating age ranges, family sizes and Sligo surnames are provided below.

Table 6. Sligo Custom and Excise Cases

1:
Mary MacCartney (80) RC. Breach of excise law October 13, 1854. Fines £12.18. Discharged November 24, 1854.

2:
John Waters (24) February 19, 1842. Conveying illicit spirits. 3 calendar months or £6. Discharged paying £4 on March 19, 1842.

John Waters(50). November 10, 1855. Illegally making malt at Innismurray on June 22, 1855. Sentence : three calendar months or £6. Discharged by order of Inland Revenue January 29, 1856. (1653/56)

John Waters(55) May 15, 1860. Private distillation at Ennismurray(sic) Island April 26, 1860. Sentence 6 months or £20 fine. Discharged on payment of fine.

Cross reference with the General Register for Sligo allows the researcher to further discover that John Waters was 5'7', with hair brown, eyes grey, eyebrows brown, nose large, mouth large. Complexion fair. Visage long. Make stout. Farmer by occupation. Born at (Cleveragh?). Residence Innismurray. Parish Ahenish. Barony Carbury. Previously in jail 3 times.

3:

Francis Gahagan (69) . 3 calendar months hard labour or pay fine £30.
Mary Gahagan (74)Manufacturing illicit tobacco. 3 calendar month hard labour or pay £30.
Michael Gahagan (28) 6 calendar months hard labour and a fine of £12.
31st January 1839.

4:

Ann E Haran (20), Catherine Haran(25) March 18 1870, found in house where illicit distillation of spirits was carrying on'.

James Barklay (16) , Margarat Barklay(53), Ellen Barklay(21) found in still house March 19 1842. Sentence served by Margarat's two children. Mother discharged by James Weir, Collector of Excise.

Peter Butler(20), Bessy Butler (15), Catherine Butler (12) found where manufacture of potale was carrying on April 18, 1843. Oldest two served 3 calendar months. Youngest discharged by Collector of Excise, P. Kelly.

James Gillon (35), Francis Gillon (60), Mary Gillon(60), Michael Gillon (18), James Gillon (12) , Hugh Gillon(10) discovered in a still house at Ballyconnell, February 25 1848. No sentence served. Discharged by commissioner.

12   ACCOUNT RELATIVE TO ILLICIT DISTILLATION (IRELAND).

AN ACCOUNT of the Number of PERSONS confined in each GAOL in *Ireland*, for Offences against the Laws for the Suppression of ILLICIT DISTILLATION, on the 5th day of January, the 5th day of March, and the 5th day of April 1845.

GAOLS.	NUMBER OF PERSONS CONFINED		
	On 5th January 1845.	On 5th March 1845.	On 5th April 1845.
Carrick-on-Shannon	10	8	6
Carrickfergus	1	1	2
Castlebar	17	30	30
Cavan	8	9	2
Clare (County)	-	-	1
Downpatrick	4	-	5
Dungannon Bridewell	-	1	1
Enniskillen	-	5	4
Galway (County)	2	7	7
Lifford	30	33	40
Limerick (County)	-	1	1
Londonderry	5	5	3
Longford	1	3	3
Maryborough	1	2	2
Monaghan	-	-	4
Mullingar	-	1	—
Omagh	9	16	12
Roscommon	3	2	2
Sligo	9	9	10
	100	133	135

Excise Office, London,
7 May 1845.

G. A. *Cottrell*,
Acc^t Genl.

Table 7.   Excise Offenders for 1845 confined in various jails. [33]

Were similar excise registers kept for other county jails as well? Inspector reports would indicate that Sligo had a particular problem with this crime, but other locations were worse. It is likely that these counties kept similar registers but they have not survived to the present day.

The general prison register for Sligo Jail survives for the years 1837- 79 and comes in three batches on the same microfilm reel.[34] October 31, 1837 - De-

---

[33] *Ibid.* 1845 (296) Spirits. Spirits (Ireland). Accounts relative to foreign and British spirits, from the year 1780 to 1844 inclusive; page 12. Accessed Dec 12, 2010. Institutional subscription required.

[34] National Archives, Dublin, MFGS 51/094.

cember 23, 1857 is a very dense register with 45 entries on each page recorded in small writing. It is in good condition, however, and can be fairly well read. Religion of the offender was recorded early, from July 1838, five years before this information was collected on the general register of Kilmainham Jail, for example . The age of the inmate was also given. On the other hand, no address or physical description was provided. From January 1ˢᵗ 1858- December 29 1879, degree of education was added but still no address. Sligo prison is one of the few jails to use the numerical notation for standard of inmate education. Few prisons in this collection observed this convention, possibly because of the danger of different clerks reversing the order over a period of time , assigning 1 to illiterate and 5 to Read and Write, which was indeed observed in the record.

Numerical system for recording education of inmate:
1. Meant Read and write.
2. Meant Read imperfectly.
3. Meant Know spelling.
4. Meant Know alphabet.
5. Meant Wholly Illiterate.

Another book of entries for 1861-1863 provides an incredible level of prisoner detail. This includes trade or calling, place of birth, residence before committal, parish, barony, county, crime, age, height, description, visage, make, marks, previous convictions, colour of hair, eyes and eyebrows, size of nose. Unfortunately, this short but invaluable record is marred by torn and missing pages.

Under the Influence
The Ennis Inebriate Reformatory

The county jail for Clare was completed in the early 1830s at a location currently occupied by Braid Mills, Station Road, Ennis. It was closed in 1880 due to lack of prisoner numbers, although it continued to operate as a remand centre. Records covering its time as the county jail have not survived. In 1899 the jail was reopened as a reform centre for alcoholic offenders on foot of the Inebriates Act of 1898 and renamed the Ennis State Inebriate Reformatory. This was an unusual hybrid of a medical and penal institution, the first of its kind in Ireland . The distinctive case books of its inmates from 1902-1920 are the only part of the archive to have been handed down to the present day . [35] Though perhaps a little late for the purposes of this project, this archive is so unusual and genealogically rich that it is worth mentioning, as many of the case histories provide a wealth of detail concerning family members . One example, that of William Head, is provided below:

Case History and Family Tree

William E. Head, (36) admitted September 1901. His file revealed that he was married but separated from his wife and had no surviving children. It revealed that his father had died twelve years ago (1888) whereupon he had succeeded to his seat at Derrylahan (Tipperary). He had been a lieutenant in the Antrim Militia, and had a brother who was a lieutenant with the 5th Dragoon Guards. His mother,

---

[35] National Archives,Dublin, MFGS 51/079.

I.E. Head, named as next of kin, was living at Moorepark, near Birr, her paternal homeland. From these salient details it was an easy matter to pinpoint and then assemble a brief pedigree of William Head :

Table 8. Brief Pedigree of William Edward Head

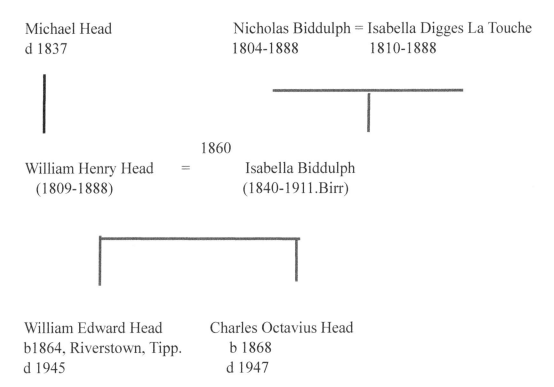

Michael Head
d 1837

Nicholas Biddulph = Isabella Digges La Touche
1804-1888   1810-1888

1860
William Henry Head   =   Isabella Biddulph
  (1809-1888)   (1840-1911.Birr)

William Edward Head   Charles Octavius Head
b1864, Riverstown, Tipp.   b 1868
d 1945   d 1947

There are a total of 292 people in the Ennis Inebriate archive . Both men and women feature , although women predominate . They came from all parts of the country. Most were in their twenties, thirties or forties as would be expected, although there was the occasional older inmate who would have been born before civil registration began. An example was 'Anne Meehan, aged 75 in 1905. Born Churchtown, Cork and said to be living at Charleville. Last abode Cork Prison. Widow. RC. Illiterate. A hunchback. No relations.' The 1901 census didn't record her.

There was an attempt by the authorities to follow up on the inmates after their treatment and discharge. The list of cases was also indexed by name for ease of research.

'Conducive to greater propriety of conduct'[36]
Grangegorman Lane Women's Prison

The women's prison for Dublin opened in 1831 on the site of the formidable old Richmond Penitentiary which was designed by Armagh-born architect, Francis Johnston . Essentially a penal experiment based on some of the suggestions of the SIPD, Grangegorman Lane was the first female-only prison in the British Isles and was presided over by a matron, Marion Rawlins, though it still had a male governor. Eighteen classes of prisoner were identified and there was greater use made of dormitory space than in male prisons. A regime of silence rather than solitary confinement was fostered . Grangegorman housed all the women subject to a custodial sentence in Dublin city as well as female convicts slated for transportation and then penal servitude after 1853. From the 1850s it kept records for untried prisoners on remand as well. Surviving records run from 1831 to 1897 over twenty-four reels of microfilm . The years 1842-43,1846-48, and 1857-63 are missing, however. Surviving records are characterized by meticu-

---

[36] Words of Marion Rawlins, Superindentent of Grangegorman Convict Prison, 8 Jan 1856. 2nd Annual Report of the Inspectors of Convict Prisons of Ireland for 1855, 1856. Eppi.http://eppi.dippam.ac.uk. Accessed June, 2013.

lous neatness and detail. There are some alphabetical name indexes available for certain years in the 1880s and 1890s.

Dominic Marques was governor of the prison in 1847. His report to the Inspectors-general that year explained that separate registers were kept for drunkards and vagrants as 'the number of such classes would utterly confuse the criminal registry'.[37] This model of record-keeping was likely to have occurred for most of the larger jails too. But they have not survived to any great extent.

Many of Grangegorman's **Registries of Drunkards** have survived to the present day, however, and they make up a unique and extensive part of this prison's collection. Over sixty thousand names were recorded, making it much more comprehensive than the equivalent for men at the Richmond Bridewell. The periods covered are : 1839-1840. 1848-1855. 1861-1869. 1875-1880. [38] There is an index of names for 1878-1880. Details on the prisoner consist of name and age initially. From July 1853, religion and educational standard were added. From 1865, place of birth was given.

It is interesting to compare the annual totals of drunkards with those for men at the Richmond Bridewell. Not only does this show that the problem of drunkenness was particularly acute for women, it also revealed that the numbers increased and declined for the same years in both cases. 1878 was the worst year for female drunkards. This may have been due to increasing rates of vagrancy as a result of the economic depression brought on by harvest failures between 1878-1879. The increase in pauperism was noted with some alarm by the inspectors in their report of the following year. [39] The large numbers at this time may also have been augmented by the Habitual Drunkards Act of 1879, which gave formal definition to an "habitual drunkard" as "*a person who not being amenable to any jurisdiction in lunacy, is, notwithstanding, by reason of habitual intemperate drinking of intoxicating liquor, at times dangerous to himself or herself or to others, is incapable of managing himself or herself, and his or her affairs.*"

---

[37] *Proquest*. House of Commons Parliamentary Papers Online. http://parlipapers.chadwyck.co.uk .1847-48 [952] Prisons of Ireland. Twenty-sixth report of the inspectors-general on the general state of the prisons of Ireland, 1847. Page 41. Accessed December 14, 2010. Institutional subscription required.

[38] National Archives, Dublin,Registry of Drunkards Grangegorman, MFGS 51/ 037,38,39.

[39] *Proquest*. House of Commons Parliamentary Papers Online. http://parlipapers.chadwyck.co.uk. 1880 [C.2689] General Prisons Board Second Report,1879-1880, page 9. Accessed May 10 ,2011.

Table 9: Annual returns in Drunkard Registries 1861-1880.

	Richmond Bridewell (males)	Grangegorman (females)
1861	532	1506
1862	584	1839
1863	830	2230
1864	1170	2424
1865	1312	2347
1866	703	1648
1867	525	1239
1868	656	1315
1869	981	1309
1870	1340	NA
1871	1105	NA
1872	583	NA
1873	124 (up to Sep 12)	NA
1874	NA	NA
1875	NA	2348
1876	NA	3462
1877	NA	3872
1878	NA	4216
1879	NA	4048

Grangegorman's **Registry of Vagrants** runs from 1850 to 1855, but with most of 1852-3 missing . [40] It is more detailed than the Drunkard Registry, giving age, religion, educational standard and place of birth from the start. The only particulars missing were occupation and physical description. Not surprisingly more family members were in evidence in this register, usually a mother and daughter . Ages ranged from eight to seventy. Thirty-three families were identified for March 1851 alone. 20 % of the sample for that month were Dublin born. 10 % could read

---

[40] National Archives, Dublin,Register of Vagrants, Grangegorman Prison. MFGS 51/039.

and write. 17% could read only. Surprisingly , March 1854 saw no improvement in the situation compared to the earlier year sampled. If anything, overall numbers had increased by 20 % with forty families identified out of a total of 452 inmates.

The general registers of Grangegorman were used to conduct a study on prison population changes between 1841 and 1851, to see what effect factors such as the Great Famine might have had. The results were interesting. Out of 549 inmates for the months of November to December in 1841, committed for a range of offences, 226 or 41% were Dublin born. 80% were Catholic. 20% were Protestant. [41] In 1851, of the 715 inmates for November to December, 34 % were Dublin born. The percentage of Catholics had risen to 87% and Protestants had declined to 13%. [42] The figures suggest a shift in population over the decade with women from neighbouring counties greatly increasing their representation in the capital. In ten years the female city prisoners had become 7 percent less urban and 7 percent less Protestant, although it was noted that the rate of non Dublin-born inmates in 1841 was higher than expected. Large numbers of inmates came from places like Summerhill, Meath, and Hacketstown, Carlow, underlining how populace these areas were at the time.

Another record unique to Grangegorman consists of those detained under the ***Habitual Criminals Act 1869***. [43] Level of detail is better here for the genealogist than in all the other prison registers, as the address of friends (usually family) and the intended address after prisoner's release was also documented. [44] In 1882, the GPB published a hardcopy register of all habitual criminals in the country, a figure in excess of eight thousand names. Although nearly two thousand copies were distributed to jails , bridewells and RIC barracks at the time , no copies appear to exist in any public repositories today . The survival of the Habitual Offenders Registers at Grangegorman, which run from 1870 to 1881, is a small compensation for this loss.

The Grangegorman archive includes a small but valuable Register of Lunatics committed from the nearby Richmond Asylum under *1st Vic., Cap. 27th* .

---

[41] Ibid, General Register Grangegorman Prison. MFGS 51/148.

[42] Ibid, General Register Grangegorman Prison. MFGS 51/029.

[43] Ibid, Register of Prisoners detained under the *Habitual Criminal Act 1869*, Apr 16 1870- Feb 10 1881. MFGS 51/148-149.

[44] Ibid, Grangegorman Registry of Prisoners under the Habitual Criminal Act 1870-1881, MFGS 51/148.

(Founded in 1815, Richmond Asylum was the oldest and largest district asylum in the country.) Dating from January 1865- December 1867, the record emphasizes the close links that existed between penal and psychiatric institutions until the latter part of the Nineteenth Century. [45] Indeed the only way lunatics could access an asylum was through committal to prison. (Excluding bridewells). This situation was amended in 1867, but many magistrates who were used to the old system continued to operate by its code.

The lunatic records were accompanied by an assessment of the prisoner's state of mind by a medical officer. They were otherwise detailed about the prisoner but gave no physical description. Reason for imprisonment ranged from 'threatened suicide' and 'assault' to the descriptive 'swinging a clergyman round by his soutane'. The 'available means of support' column - another unique feature of this record- is genealogically useful since it often names a father, mother, or son. Prisoner movement was in the other direction too , from prison to asylum, with those committed to Grangegorman and then found insane after committal. This record goes up to 1894. There are a total of 356 people in this collection, including some men from 1878. (From 1874, a wing of Grangegorman had been set aside for male petty offenders.)

---

[45] Ibid, Grangegorman Register of Lunatics committed from Richmond Asylum MFGS 51/140

No.	NAMES	Age.	When Committed. 1848	By Whom Committed.	Sentence.	Fine.	When Discharged.	General Observations.
2051	Jane Price	24	8th Augt	H. Callaghan Esq.	24 HOURS	1/6	9 Augt	
"	Emily Thompson	16				1/6	"	
3	Agnes Fox	27				1/6	"	
4	Mary A Wilson	23				1/6	"	
5	Ellen Raynor	36	9th	Geo. Hyre Esq.		1/	10th	
6	Mary A Mathews	21	"			1/6		
7	Sarah Walker	56						
8	Cathe Masterson	17		S W Purcell Esq		2/6		
9	Sarah Nolan	24				1/6		
2060	Maria Crotie	16				1/		
1	Anne Flanagan	16				2/		
2	Ellen Bourke	40				2/6		
3	Ellen Reed	15				1/		
4	Harriet Doolan	16	10th	Geo. Hyre Esq	24	1/6	11th	
5	Ellen Gore	13		J L Crump Esq	24	1/	11th	
6	Alicia Kavanagh	20				1/		

Table 10: *Sample of Grangegorman Register of Drunkards for 1848*

'Eager to draw attention to everything he considered a defect' [46]
Tralee Jail

Built in 1812 about a quarter of a mile from the town at Bullymullen, be-side the infantry barracks, Tralee Jail served as both county jail and remand centre for those brought up for the assizes. The 1851 Census Report for Ireland revealed that it had the worst epidemic death rate of all jails in Munster. [47] The Inspector's report of 1867 was also critical of its 'flagrantly defective construction'. Tralee jail was built in the shape of a cross, making it unable to fulfill the demands of the Victorian prisoner classification credo. The prison fell into disuse after 1923. Little of the structure now remains except for the perimeter walls.

Tralee's surviving records are spread over three microfilms in the National Archives, Dublin. They commence on June 1852 and run continuously to the end of 1866. [48] There is a large gap at this point with the general register not resuming until November 1888, although an alphabetical index of inmates' names is avail-

---

[46] Thomas Reid,*Travels in Ireland in the Year 1822,* page 287. Longman, Hurst, Rees, Orme, and Brown, 1823. (Observation by author on the prison assistant who gave him a guided tour of Tralee gaol.)

[47] *Proquest*. House of Commons Parliamentary Papers Online. http://parlipapers.chadwyck.co.uk. 1856 [2087-I] [2087-II] The census of Ireland for the year 1851. Part V. Tables of deaths. Vol. II. Page 125. Accessed April 4, 2011. Institutional subscription required.

[48] National Archives, Dublin,MFGS 51/099

able from 1879. [49] (This index also gives age and occasionally occupation. Debtors are also specified. There is no index for 1883, probably because the next prison year was to start on April 1st ,1884. This system was seen in other prisons as well, but with the exception of Castlebar , it was quickly abandoned, presumably because it was found impractical.) For many of those missing years in the records the Petty Sessions order books for Tralee are available in the National Archives[50] and online. [51]

The early Tralee general register ,1852-1866, was written up in neat and beautiful handwriting. But it gave little prisoner information other than name, age, crime, where and when tried and verdict . At no time was religion, address, trade or physical description provided, which means Tralee lags well behind other county jails for the period. This format remained largely unchanged for the length of the record , though from February 1859 the clerk specified the previous number of times a prisoner entered the jail. Aliases were also given when applicable. Debtors were recorded but , unlike most county prisons, the sum of the debt wasn't specified. A possible reason for the deficiency is that Tralee may well have used a separate register, a so-called **description register**, to record more prisoner details. This system was seen to be used in this survey by one of its nearest neighbours, Cork County Jail. [52]

There were a great deal of begging cases when the record begins in 1852 and they form the largest class of offender for that year. For July alone there were 36 (20%) begging cases out of a total of 176 offences of all kinds. Whole families, in many cases parents and large numbers of children, were brought into custody together. Begging was the most familial offence on the register and there was a high level of reoffending . A month in jail was the usual sentence.

Some cases of begging from Tralee Jail, 1852.

Norry Moriarty (35), Daniel Moriarty (12), John Moriarty (9), Ellen Moriarty (14), Norry Moriarty(½), Mary Moriarty (10) charged with begging January 31 1853.

---

[49] Ibid , MFGS 51/ 099-100.

[50] Ibid, MFGS 58/ 2772-4.

[51] findmypast.ie. Subscription required.

[52] National Archives, Cork County Gaol Description Register, MFGS 51/ 023.

All received a calendar month in jail. The same family are brought up again in March 16, 1853 and received the same sentence. There was no sign of Daniel the second time round.

Murty Sullivan (60), Margaret Sullivan (45), Judith Sullivan (17), Johanna Sullivan (16), Michael Sullivan (14), Mary Sullivan (4 ½) charged with begging June 28, 1852. One calendar month in jail.

By 1862, there were only nineteen crimes involving families out of a total of 649. (3%). This compares with 6% for 1852. It might be deduced from this that the further the records advance from the Famine years, the smaller the proportion of cases involving entire families.

Unusual names which did not feature in prisons from other regions in-cluded Lucid (said to be a variation of Lucey[53], though Maclysaght prefers the explanation that it is a gaelicized version of Lucas), Allman, Broder and Brick. Other names peculiar to the area included Pellican, Tangney and Kerrisk. Typical local names such as Sullivan, Connor , MacCarthy and Moriarty abounded and it might be concluded that the prison population tended to be very local. This gave rise to some analysis of the relative numerical strength of certain surnames. A sur-vey of Sullivan numbers in the jail over ten years was undertaken.

Table 11: Sullivan Survey at Tralee Jail

Year	Total Sullivans	Total entries	Total O'Sullivans
1852:	112	942 entries (From June 1852.)	0
1853:	141	1969	0
1854:	168	1386	2 (Both Debtors)
1855:	99	916	2 (One a Debtor)
1856:	43	682	0
1857:	57	815	0

---

[53] Michael C. O'Laughlin, *Families of County Kerry, Ireland.* Irish Genealogical Foundation, Kan-sas Missouri, 1994. Page 93.

1858:	62	799	0
1859:	45	554	0
1860:	35	561	0
1861:	58	649	1 (A Debtor)
1862:	46	649	0
Totals:	866	9922	5

The survey shows that Sullivans averaged 8.73 % of the prison population annually over the ten years. Virtually none used the 'O' prefix. Curiously, a disproportionate number of those who who did were debtors.

Table 12: Study of Total Rate of 'O' prefixes on various surnames.

Year	Number of 'O' prefixes	Name
1853	1	O'Brien
1854	2	O'Sullivan
	1	O'Donnell
	2	O'Connor (1 a debtor)
	1	O'Halloran (debtor)
	1	O'Brien
1855	2	O'Sullivan (debtor)
	1	O'Callaghan
	1	O'Brien
1856	2	O'Brien
	1	O'Connor
	1	O'Connell (debtor)
1857	2	O'Brien
	2	O'Connor(1 a debtor)
	1	O'Donnell
	1	O'Donohue
	1	O'Flaherty(debtor)
1858	3	O'Brien
	1	O'Connor (a debtor)
	1	O'Connell

1859	4	O'Brien
	1	O'Donnell
	1	O'Gready
1860	3	O'Brien
1861	1	O'Hagan
	1	O'Gready
	1	O'Riordan
	1	O'Sullivan
1862	1	O'Meally
1863	1	O'Brien
	2	O'Connor (both debtors)
	2	O'Sullivan
Total	45	

In terms of prefix breakdown, O'Brien took 40%. O'Connor 18%. O'Sullivan 16%. 20% of the 'O' prefix users were debtors. Although this is substantially less than the rates found in Robert Matheson's surname study in 1890, where 67 % of O'Briens were reported to use the prefix, the relative proportions are in line, with the prefix for O'Brien being roughly twice that for O'Connor. In contrast to this, Mc(Mac)Cart(h)y far outnumbered Cart(h)y in the prison records, as did Mc(Mac)Mahon vis a vis Mahon. A brief survey was done on the Shea surname, the fifty-eighth commonest surname in Ireland today. [54] There were 193 estimated over the ten years with not a single individual using the 'O' prefix. (The rate was 14 % in Matheson's Survey.) Almost the reverse is true today with 98 % of Sheas preferring the 'O' prefix. There were 72 Moriartys in the prison survey compared with 193 Sheas, a ratio that mirrors their relative numerical strength in the GRO of 1890 for Munster. (79 as against 217)[55]

     A useful feature of the Tralee register was that from 1894 **Irish-speaking offenders** were noted in the margin, seven years before the 1901 Census of Ireland provided this information officially.

---

[54] Sean J. Murphy, 'A Survey of Irish Surnames 1992-97 (Draft)', Appendix 1, *Studies in Irish Genealogy and Heraldry*, 2009, page 26, http://homepage.eircom.net/~seanjmurphy/studies/surnames.pdf. Accessed June 1, 2011.

[55] Sir Robert E. Matheson, *A Special Report on the Surnames of Ireland with notes as to Numerical strength etc.* Alex Thom & Co., Dublin. 1909, Page 65 &71.

A Century of Penal Records
Kilmainham

Opened in 1796 to replace an older jail, Kilmainham was considered the most up to date prison of its era. [56] Throughout its long history it served as the county jail for Dublin, a remand centre for those awaiting trial and a convict depot for the entire country. Each category of prisoner is liberally represented in its records. George Dunn (died Nov 25, 1841), a turnkey since the time of Robert Emmet, was the long-time governor of the jail. By 1830 the jail had fallen down to third class category in the government inspector's reports, due mainly to its failure to provide work facilities for inmates. [57] This opinion reflected the trend away from hard labour towards productive industrial labour on the part of penal administrators. The report of 1842 described it as 'an ill-constructed gaol and much retarded in discipline by the detention in it of Government Convicts'. [58]

---

[56] Tim Carey. *Mountjoy- the Story of a Prison*, page 22. Collins Press. 2000.

[57] *Proquest*. House of Commons Parliamentary Papers Online. http://parlipapers.chadwyck.co.uk 1830 (48) Prisons of Ireland. Eighth Report of the Inspectors General on the General State of the Prisons of Ireland: 1830 Page 25 . Accessed December 23, 2010. Institutional subscription required.

[58] *Ibid,* 1842 842 [377] Prisons of Ireland. Twentieth report of the inspectors general on the general state of the prisons of Ireland, 1841. Page 127. Accessed Feb 16 2011.

The opening of Smithfield convict depot in 1845 relieved this situation. In the 1840s the jail was made more comfortable with the installation of gas and glazed windows. The more modern horse-shoe shaped east wing of ninety-six cells was completed in 1861 . It reflected the key principles of Nineteenth Century prison reform - silence, industry and separation. Kilmainham was the scene of the last public hanging in Dublin, that of Patrick Kilkenny on July 22,1865.[59]

With a starting date of April 20, 1797, Kilmainham has both the oldest and the longest surviving prison registers in the country. With the exception of the missing years 1824-1830, the jail's general registers are virtually intact up to 1910. The first pages are devoted to treason felony offenders relating to 1798 and the Emmet rebellion of 1803. The general register, which is separate from the treason felon list, commences on January 29, 1799. Given its age it is reasonably easy to read, if a little faint. Unfortunately the register doesn't provide prisoner age , address or occupation at this time. There is simply a name, date of committal, crime, sentence and process of discharge. 386 prisoners were recorded in 1799, of which 37 were debtors.

Early Record of Heights

From 1803 a separate register recorded the age and,unusually, the height of a prisoner, calculated to the half inch. Some prisoners in this book were treason felony cases. Indeed the purpose of recording heights may have arisen from a need for better identification in the event of rebellion. Whatever the cause of this initiative, all other classes of prisoner, including debtors, had their heights recorded subsequently when they entered the gaol. The height of female offenders was set down from 1804. This is perhaps the oldest record of the heights of a fairly large group of Dublin dwellers. The practice peters out in August 1813, but by then the stature of 2826 prisoners had been set down, 2554 men and 265 women. (One child, a fourteen year old, was excluded from the survey.)

A total of 32 men (1.25%) were 6 foot tall and over. The tallest two were jointly Michael Cullen, 28, 6'1' , Feb 7 1809, possession of mutton and wool, and William O'Connor, 54, 6'1' , 27 Nov 1810, suspicion of felony. Of the 32 six footers, three (9%) were soldiers and five (16%) were debtors.

---

[59] Tim Carey . *Mountjoy- the Story of a Prison*. Collins Press. 2000. Page 156.

The results for women were surprising. Of the 265 women found in this collection (roughly 10% of the total) only one was found to be under five feet : Catherine Mullen, 25, 4'10', a convict from Westmeath. The majority, 142 of the 265 (or 52%) were 5'5' (1.65 m) , a height which would not be out of place in contemporary Ireland. (A survey on Irish eating habits in 2001 recorded the heights of 662 men and 717 women. The average heights were 1.75 (5'9') metres for men and 1.62 (5'4') metres for women aged 18-64.[60]) 17% of the Kilmaiham women were 5'6'. 16% were 5'4'. Only 6% were 5'7'. The tallest was Mary Ann Vickery, 35, 5'10', a debtor. Unless this sample is especially unrepresentative, the findings suggest that a tall, well-fed population came to maturity in early 1800s Dublin, although it can't be assumed because of lack of data on birthplace that those surveyed were Dubliners.

Cormac O'Grada of UCD has made a similar study of the heights of Clonmel Jail inmates, albeit for a larger group and a later generation, 1845 and 1849. [61] He argues that there was a high correlation at the time between literacy levels, and therefore income, and height. His findings support the thesis that Irishmen were taller than their British counterparts in the pre-Famine era. Available data tended to show that the population of Leinster was smaller than for other provinces but the findings for the women of Kilmainham conflict with this view, since their average height was nine centimetres taller than that of the Clonmel females.

Table 13.

Kilmainham Heights (Women) 1804-1813

Sample size: 265.
Minimum: 1.47
Maximum:1.78
Average: 1.65
Average deviation: 0.02

---

[60] North/South Ireland Food Consumption Survey. Irish Universities Nutrition Alliance. Summary Report. 2001. Page 17. Food Safety Promotion Board, Abbey Court, Lower Abbet Street, Dublin 1.

[61] Research_Online@UCD, Cormac O'Grada. 'Heights in Tipperary in the 1840s : evidence from prison
registers'. *Ir. Econ. Soc. Hist. XVIII(1991)*, page 24-33. Accessed June 20th 2011.

O'Grada Survey (Women) 1841-1849
Sample Size: 558
Minimum 1.54
Maximum 1.58
Average: 1.56

From 1843, an important genealogical development occurred when the form of the register provided designated columns for religion, marital status, education and trade. Then from June 1846 , **native place** was also added. This puts Kilmainham ahead of many county jails which provided this last piece of information from the early 1860s only . The increase in committals over the following years is telling. (These figures are provided by the registers themselves, not the official reports.)

Kilmainham Commitals from 1844-1849
1844 - 1286
1845 - 1267
1846 - 1265 of which 444 female.
1847 - 2551
1848 - 4655, of which 446 were drunkards and 1917 were vagrants. (Almost equal to the total number of prisoners committed between 1803 and 1815.)
1849 - 6888, of which only 1802 were actually written in on the register, 4652 were beggars, 368 drunkards.

The summary for 1849 shows that the vast majority of those who entered the jail were not recorded in the general register at all . One explanation was inundation. Another explanation is that a separate register was kept for beggars and drunkards, as is hinted at by the governor of Grangegorman in the inspectors report of 1847. If so, the destruction of these books for Kilmainham represents a great loss. Throughout this period there was an indexed list of recommittals for 1845, divided into males and females. There is also a useful alphabetical index of names for the year 1846. In terms of general registers, Kilmainham has the best coverage of the Famine years of all the Dublin jails investigated.

In the late 1860s the jail adopted the practice of recording the **names of babies and toddlers** who accompanied their mothers to prison. This was not a widespread practice for county jails. (Tralee, Castlebar and Naas never give a child's name for instance.) Kilmainham ended up catering mainly for petty male offenders in its last years. It was wound down and closed by the General Prisons Board in 1910, only to be reopened under extraordinary circumstances in 1916.

'The Most perfect institution of its kind in Ireland'[62]
Cork County Jail

Located off the Western Road, Cork, about three quarters of a mile from the city, little remains of the Cork County Jail's original structure, which was demolished in 1960 except for the south wall and its doric pillars. Designed by the English-born Pain Brothers, George and James, in 1818 , Cork County Jail incorporated the so-called **House of Correction** , a throw back to a Tudor penal system in which solitary confinement and hard labour were meted out to petty offenders and vagrants. [63]To this end it was equipped with tread wheels and isolation cells .

Surviving records run over twenty reels of microfilm with a start date of 1819 . They provide ample evidence of the agrarian unrest which reached its peak in 1821-22. These activities were widespread in counties Tipperary, Galway , Limerick and Westmeath as well , but since prison records don't exist for the appropriate dates in these particular counties, Cork County Jail provides perhaps the best first hand prison archive on this topic. The passing of the **Insurrection Act** in 1822 made association of groups illegal and facilitated the sentencing of so-called Whiteboys to transportation. The jail's own returns for 1822 reveal that 205 cases were prosecuted under the Insurrection Act alone. Not surprisingly, many family members , or at least individuals of the same surname, were prosecuted under the act.

---

[62] *The Penny Cyclopædia of the Society for the Diffusion of Useful Knowledge*, Volume 8, page 16. C. Knight, 1837. Google Books.

[63] www.londonlives.org/static/HousesOfCorrection.jsp. Accessed June 2013.

An unusual offence dating from this period relates to those prosecuted under the **Green Wax Process**. This was an offence against an Exchequer fine, issued by the County Sheriff , which was delivered on a parchment sealed with green wax. The offence was deemed important enough to be given its own column under annual jail totals even though the perpetrators were few. Unlike Cork City Gaol, debtors are named in the early registers, although the sum of their debt was usually left out.

Cork County Jail provides better coverage of the Famine years than the city jail at Sunday's Well, although throughout this period the only personal details recorded continued to be the name and age of the prisoner. At the end of every year the clerk provided a table of totals broken down by gender and types of offences. This practice was abandoned in 1847 , the year that saw an explosive increase in prison numbers - 5320 compared to 1562 for 1846. It wasn't until 1875 that the end of year table returned.

In 1853 there was a major improvement in register format with full physical description, education, religion, birth place, and trade or calling given. [64] An added bonus for the researcher is that the married state of prisoner was also recorded from 1853-1860 under what appears to have been the local administrator's own initiative, as there was no designated column for this detail. The trade or calling column was frequently left blank in this period, however.

By 1870 the clerk stopped filling in physical description, marital status, birth place and occupation. Why the deterioration in record-keeping? The likely reason is that Cork County Jail used a separate book called a **Description Register** to record detailed personal information. This register, which only seems to have survived for Cork, runs from 1870 to 1878.[65] It includes a detailed physical description, birthplace, an address, and intended address after release. Relations are often identified in the "friends at" column. From December 9, 1878, males and females are put in separate registers.

---

[64] National Archives, MFGS 51/ 010.

[65] National Archives, Description Registers Cork County Jail, MFGS 51/023-24.

'The Women's Jail'
Cork City Jail

Built on elevated ground at Sunday's Well in 1824 to replace the hundred year old city jail at Northgate Bridge, Cork City Jail was designed by Thomas Deane in a distinctive castellated style. It was built to cater for all prisoners whose crimes were committed within the city boundary of Cork. The long-time governor was the popular John Barry Murphy. Re-modelled in 1870, it became exclusively a women's prison in 1878 . It was remembered long after that on the day of transfer the men were marched out of Sunday's Well Prison and over to the County Gaol off Western Road, while the women were marched in the opposite direction into Sunday's Well. [66]The jail was closed in 1923 and is preserved as a museum today.

Surviving records are not as extensive as those for Cork County jail and cover convicted prisoners only. They cover the years 1823-1878, running over five reels of microfilm at the National Archives, but with substantial gaps. [67]For instance the key years 1845-1848 are missing, the entire 1850s and the period extending from 1864 until most of 1870. Compensating for this there is a very well preserved index available for 1833 to 1841 with debtors given a large "D" beside their name. [68] However, debtors don't appear on the general register up until 1844, when unfortunately the archive is interrupted. There are no women to be found in the register either. When the surviving registers resume in 1848 both classes of

---

[66] Cork City Jail Heritage Centre, http://corkcitygaol.com/about/history/, Accessed July 2013.

[67] National Archives, MFGS 51/010-14.

[68] National Archives, MFGS 51/ 010.

prisoner are in evidence. Unlike the county jail, the sum of the debtor's debt is recorded.

Information to be found in the general records from the start include name, age, crime, date of committal and place of residence (broken into parish or town and county). [69] From 1833 the clerk stopped filling in the place of residence, replacing this information the following year with information on fines and costs and the length of a prisoner's sentence. There is a remarks column also which is diligently filled in with details on the prisoner's behaviour in jail until 1828, after which time it is left blank. The microfilmed copy for the period 14 Sep, 1828-13 Apr, 1829 is faded and virtually unreadable. Apart from that the surviving records are in good condition. The prisoner's educational standard was included from 1838.

The clerk wrote in the totals for each type of offence at the end of every year . There was a noticeable lack of drunkard cases, always less than ten annually. The single biggest category involved assault, followed by military offences. Inmate totals were smaller for the city jail, for example 635 as against the county jail's 1055 in 1837.

The city jail records are augmented by **court journals** running from 1830 to 1839 and 1847 to 1848. [70] These fill in some of the gaps evident in the prison registers proper. The court journals are a little fainter and harder to read than the jail registers but they give information on whether the prisoner was tried at assizes or the petty sessions , naming the location, for example Kanturk assizes, and so revealing prisoner's likely origins . The prisoner's age is included from 1834 onwards and level of education from 1847 onwards.

---

[69] Ibid.

[70] National Archives, MFGS 51/ 013-14.

'The person is for ever released, but the property never... '[71]
Debtors' Records

Debtors were the only class of prisoner that the penal system set out to punish by detention. This is reflected in the fact that of the nine prisons operating in Dublin in the Eighteenth and Nineteenth Centuries, five were exclusively devoted to debtors. [72] These included the Sheriff's Prison (closed in the 1840s) and Marshalsea, (reserved for the few imprisoned by the Court of Conscience or Lord Mayor's Court).Both were based near Newgate , St. Mary's Abbey. There were also the Four Courts Marshalsea (closed in 1874), St Sepulchre's Manor, (Kevin Street) and Smithfield Depot.

Few if any of debtors' prison records have survived, however. Of all class of prisons, the debtor's prisons were undeniably the worst run and with little central supervision. A valuable list of debtors in Dublin jails between 1730-31 appeared in the *Dublin Gazette* and is reproduced by the *Dublin Historical Record.*[73] It gives particulars such as name, address and trade. An equivalent list of fifty-five names for Cork city is available too.[74]

---

[71] Google Books, http://books.google.com Samuel Leigh . *Leigh's New Picture of London.* Leigh and Co. 1839, page 45.

[72]Jane Lyon. http://myhome.ispdr.net.au/~mgrogan/cork/jane_prison.htm. 1999. Accessed Oct 31 2010.

[73] Patrick O'Connor, *Dublin Historical Record.* Vol. 6,No. 2 (Mar.-May 1944), pages 75-80 ; Vol. 6,No. 4 (Sep.-Nov. 1944), pages 157-159.

[74] Michael V. Conlon, 'Debtors in Cork Gaols - 1705-1872', *Journal of the Cork Historical & Archaeological Society.* No. 47 1942, page 10-11.

Another surviving list is the **Kilmainham Jail** register of debtors covering the period from August 11, 1845 to September 27, 1881. [75] The record is reasonably legible although legal terms, often in Latin, make it less user-friendly. The total number of names on the Kilmainham list is 1559 . As the Nineteenth Century progressed, county jails catered increasingly for debtors by providing designated marshalseas on their grounds. Debtors' lists exist for Sligo, Cork, Limerick and Nenagh jails and it is likely that all county jails kept this type of record but they have not survived .

Like most debtor registers, Kilmainham's list differs markedly from general prison registers in format and detail. The researcher will find the name of debtor, date committed, amount of debt, at whose suit committed, class of debtor , when discharged and remarks. But they will find no address, age, or occupation. In some cases the name of the plaintiff or creditor can help to pinpoint debtor's identity or sphere of activity. The process by which the debtor is committed may also be revealing. Eg City of Dublin Decree, Mary's Abbey Decree, Grangegorman Decree. Mention of a Coroner's Execution process is significant as it can provide important clues to the death of a party.

The debtor was divided into two classes - master or pauper. The pauper debtor was dependent on the county for his maintenance in jail and had to undertake work to pay for the upkeep. Debtors could go from master to pauper over a period of time. Other processes by which the debtor was committed included:

A: **Queen's Bench** (the court dealing with offences against the 'Queen's Peace', which could be either civil or criminal .)

B: **Exchequer Bench** (revenue cases usually)

C: **Seneschal Decree** (the Seneschal was a legally trained official appointed by the Archbishop of Dublin to preside over courts and market juries of the Liberty section of Dublin[76]).

D: **Judge's Fiat** (court order by a judge).

E : **Court of Common Pleas** (had jurisdiction over real estate and civil cases). A more expensive and slower court than the Queen's Bench.

F: **Chancery Attachment** (Equity cases. Rarer in the debtors' records).

---

[75] National Archives Dublin . MFGS 51/050.

[76] *Proquest*. House of Commons Parliamentary Papers Online. http://parlipapers.chadwyck.co.uk. Vol. 24. Corporations Ireland. Vol. 24 , 1836, page 294. Accessed October 23, 2010. Institutional subscription required.

In Dublin and Cork the enforcement of civil court orders was the responsibility of a government-appointed sheriff. The commonest process of debt discharge in the Kilmainham register was through the Court of Insolvency. This was a non-jury court run by government-appointed commissioners . It allowed a debtor, after a reasonable period of imprisonment, to apply for release if he surrendered all his possessions, except his clothes and tools, to his creditors. The mechanism was summed up by the well-known phrase: 'The person is for ever released, but the property never, as long as any claims remain unsatisfied.' [77]

1848 stands out as the worst year for insolvents in Ireland, with 136 cases in Kilmainham. (The previous year's total had been 17 and the year after that 66.) This trend was duplicated in all the other surviving Irish records studied but, unlike vagrancy, begging and robbery, insolvency saw a dramatic tailing off in 1849.

Table 14: comparing debtor numbers for the various county jails.

Jail	1847	1848	1849
Limerick	490	626	137
Sligo	286	308	67
Dublin (Kilmainham)	17	136	66
Cork County Jail *	238	273	121
Nenagh	415	473	116

(*Figures derived from general register of Cork County Jail. [78])

---

[77] *Google Books*, http://books.google.com,Samuel Leigh . *Leigh's New Picture of London.* Leigh and Co. 1839, page 45.

[78] National Archives Cork County Jail MFGS 51/009.

In 1864 the automatic jailing of debtors was abolished in certain circumstances (**Small Debtors Discharge Act 1864**)[79]. This situation was consolidated by further legislation in the 1870s, and a steep decline in prison debtors was observed after the 1864 watershed. In 1873, the Queen's Bench, Chancery , Exchequer and Common Plea courts, all of which had their origins in Medieval law, were merged into the High Court.

It is surprising who turns up in the Kilmainham register. Isaac Butt (1813-1879), MP, QC and the father of the Home Rule movement ,was perhaps the worst offender in the entire archive, owing 28 plaintiffs an eye-watering total of £6731. All debts were discharged on dates between March and July 1868 through either the prison governor or the sheriff . The identity of his many creditors is revealed in this archive.

Men of the cloth were not immune either. In 1854, Reverend Joseph Hargleton Thomas was jailed for owing £5000 to Henrietta Sarah Hargrove. Later that month he provided bail to the tune of £1080 with the proviso that he was not to "withdraw himself to foreign parts without the special license of her Majesty".

The Kilmainham debt records were found not to be particularly familial. There were few instances of members of the same surname being brought to court or appearing in the same suit. An attempt was made to study this list in conjunction with the records of the Registry of Deeds(ROD) in Dublin, in order to reveal further family relationships . Since a debtor might be forced to offload leases around the year of insolvency, this could provide a useful finding aid to significant entry dates in the ROD. This exercise yielded rich results in some cases but it was by no means commonplace for those in the Debtor's book to turn up in the ROD. However, if it such was the case Pauper debtors were more likely to feature in the ROD than master debtors.

Debtors were found in great numbers in the general prison registers of nearly all county jails, where they consistently made up between 8 and 12 % of the jail population from the 1820s to the 1840s. In the case of Kilmainham Jail's general register, debtor entries become increasingly easy to spot as they are fainter than the rest, suggesting a different colour pen was used by the registrar. However there was rarely any attempt to fill in the descriptive column, prisoner's religion, marital status, trade or native place. Standard of education column and debtor's

---

[79] *Proquest*. House of Commons Parliamentary Papers Online. http://parlipapers.chadwyck.co.uk 19th Century House of Commons Sessional Papers, Vol. 11 . 1864. Page 353. Accessed Feb 15 2011. Institutional subscription required.

age were sometimes given. Since their offence was civil rather than criminal, debtors were not supposed to be subject to the prison regime. They had different food and quarters and could wear their own clothes. Nonetheless, in 1809 a parliamentary report criticised Governor Dunn of Kilmainham for his tyrannical, oppressive attitude to debtors.[80] And in 1848 the Inspector of Prisons was dismayed to discover a debtor being made to use the treadwheel at Monaghan jail. Under legislation, *Act 7, Geo.IV., cap. 74,* debtors were to be kept away from other classes of prisoner, although some county jails, notably Kerry's Tralee, failed to comply with this directive.[81]

A substantial debtor record survives for **Cork County Jail** for the years 1858- 1872.[82] The collection consists of 653 names. There are between thirty and fifty cases each year with a spike in the early 1860s of between 61 and 68 cases, mirroring the situation in Dublin. The Cork debtor records are greatly boosted for the Eighteenth Century by the records of a charitable society set up by Henry Sheares in 1774 to help small debtors. Two reports of the Relief and Discharge of Persons Society, 1775 and 1783, are available at the Royal Irish Academy. [83]

Another extensive list of debtors is found for **Sligo Jail** for the years 1843 to 1878.[84] This archive consists of 1492 names. The record is clear and legible, though there are a few missing pages at the start. Unlike the Dublin and Cork records, the debtor's religion was always given. The legal process used in Sligo was usually a Barrister's Decree or a *Capius ad Satisfaciondum*, a writ issued on foot of a civil judgment that enabled a plaintiff to have a defendant jailed until a debt was paid. [85]

---

[80] *Ibid,* 1809 (265) (Ireland.) Report from the commissioners appointed to inquire into and inspect the condition and government of the state prisons and other gaols in Ireland. Accessed Mar 17, 2011.

[81] Proquest, HCPP online, Appendix to Forty-Sixth Report of Inspector General of Prisons for Ireland, page 316.

[82] National Archives, Dublin, MFGS 51/025.

[83] Michael V. Conlon, 'Debtors in Cork Gaols - 1705-1872', *Journal of the Cork Historical & Archaeological Society.* No. 47 1942, page 15.

[84] National Archives, Dublin,MFGS 51/163.

[85] New Jersey Law Revison Commission.'Relating to Civil Arrest Capias ad Respondendum et Satisfaciendum'. Final Report. 1997 page 1-5. http://www.lawrev.state.nj.us. Accessed November 12 2010.

Most of the Sligo debts were small, a matter of a few pounds, though there was the occasional large sum. Names typical of the Sligo area, such as McGetrick, Tivnan, (a regional variation of Teevan or Teehan), Currid and Sharket were in evidence. Sligo's debtor records are more valuable from a genealogical point of view as there was a larger proportion of obvious cases involving families, with people of the same surname, likely brothers or fathers and sons, owing money to the same creditors. There were also several instances where debtors and creditors had the same surname and were possibly related. This was also seen in the Cork archive.

The longest surviving unbroken record for imprisoned debtors belongs to **Limerick Jail**, stretching from 1835 to 1881.[86] With well over six thousand names recorded, it is by far the largest archive of its kind as well as being the best preserved and legible. It broadly follows the format of the Sligo archive, but gives religion and age of debtor from 1868 only.

Debtor records for **Nenagh Jail** extend from 1843 to 1872.[87]They are also in pristine condition. Like Sligo they recorded religious persuasion from the beginning, while also providing the extra information of the debtor's standard of education. It was interesting to note that in 1843, 45 out of the total of 48 debtors could write.

Case Histories relating to Debtors' Records

1. Saunders Carroll, a debtor committed to Kilmainham Jail by Exchequer Execution on August 20 1847, found in the Registry of Deeds two years before to have been a druggist in South Great George's Street, engaged to an Ellen Lewis whose mother was Maria Lewis, otherwise O'Donoghue, a widow , of Russell Place. [88] The deed involved an entail which almost certainly contributed to Carroll's bankruptcy.

2. Sligo Jail: John Tivnan (RC) , James Tivnan(RC) , April 25 1848. Owe £12.9.6 to Sir Robert Gore Booth. Discharged by …..R Gethin, plaintiff agent. Griffith's

---

[86] National Archives, Dublin, MFGS 51/078. Limerick Jail Debtors' List. 19 Sep 1835 -14 May 1850. 22 May 1849- 28 Feb 1881.

[66] Ibid, MFGS 51/092.

[88] Registry of Deeds, King's Inn, Dublin. 1845-20-83.

Valuation records a John Tivnan as occupier of two parcels of land at Rossinver leased by Robert Gore Booth . [89] It is likely that this is the same individual mentioned in the debtor's list and may relate to unpaid rent from the earlier period. Many of the plaintiffs are agents acting on behalf of landlords , typically Gore Booth and Edward Crofton. Gore Booth features particularly prominently as a creditor.

3. John McDonagh (RC). Writ of attachment. June 28, 1853. Contempt in not performing a …(?) order in the matter of estate of John McDonagh, owner and Thomas McDonagh, petitioner. Discharged by sheriff September 21, 1853.

4. Sligo Jail: Bartholomew McGetrick (RC). July 8 1858. Creditors Andrew Bagot, John Bagot, Charles Edward Hutton. £23. 17.6. Discharged as insolvent. Remanded for three months from October 1858 at the suit of John McMayan? Snr and Jnr, trustees for Catherine McGetrick. (In 1851 a Bartholomew McGetrick married a Catherine Kilcullen, parish of Sligo.[90]) None of the other creditors are listed in available sources for Sligo, suggesting they are not local. A search in the Register of Deeds, King's Inn, for 1857, revealed that Bartholomew McGetrick was a licensed publican, Radcliffe Street Sligo, and sold his furniture and fittings at that time to a Pat McGetrick, shopman and tenant on the premises, likely a brother . [91]

---

[89] *Origins.* Griffith's *Valuation* for Sligo , Irish Origins, http://www.origins.net/IrishOrigins/Search/Census/Griffiths. Accessed December 21 2010. Commercial site.

[90] Irish Family History Foundation, www.rootsireland.ie, Marriage of Bartholomew McGetrick Sligo 1851. Accessed November 10, 2010. Commercial site.

[91] Registry of deeds, King's Inn, Dublin. Memorial (McGetrick to McGetrick, Sligo) 1857-16 -130.

'A Sad Evil'
Newgate Gaol

Designed by Thomas Cooley in 1781, Newgate was the city jail for Dublin. But from the beginning, official reports referred to its defects as a "sad evil" that would prove difficult to remedy. For a start, the area was too populace and low-lying. The jail hadn't its own water supply and there was no room for expansion to meet Nineteenth Century prisoner classification needs. In spite of these flaws, Newgate survived until well into the 1860s. The onset of the Famine revived its prominence, as did the Suspension of the Habeus Corpus Act in 1849, which led to treason felons being interned there.

Available records for Newgate cover the period when it was a remand centre for untried felons only, both men and women, and subsequently a convict depot after transportation ceased. They run over four microfilms at the National Archives. [92] The felon register covers an almost unbroken period between January 1845 to June 1858 . The convict register spans the years 1855-1861 for males and 1857- 1858 for females.

As a result, large classes of prisoners are missing from this archive. There are no drunkards, vagrants or beggars, for instance. And although Newgate was selected to hold debtors committed by coroner's decree, there is no sign of this class either. The records deal predominantly with theft or larceny cases. Watches, shoes, cloaks, tobacco, books , furniture and food feature prominently. There is the added bonus of a useful column identifying the person whose property was stolen. Some assaults and the occasional murder or manslaughter feature also. Army desertion cases are plentiful. Another useful feature from the start is that if the female felon has a child, the name and age of the child is invariably recorded

---

[92] National Archives Dublin. MFGS 51/ 067-070

in the margin. (By comparison, Kilmainham, the county jail, didn't start this practice until the 1860s.) Apart from that there is a notable lack of families evident in the register. As is the case with many other jails, it is assault cases that bring in most relatives together, but oddly there is a tendency for the clerk to fill in fewer details in these instances, leaving key particulars such as address, description and place of birth blank.

The earliest register is very damaged with what is described as "fungus growth". This situation continues from January to March 1845. After this it improves to the extent that names can be read easily but not addresses or descriptions . By November 1845 there is little damage , the writing itself is bold and clear and remains legible for the remainder of the archive. 1847 shows the largest peak in prisoner numbers after which time there is a quick decline. (No doubt because of the authorities' wish to close the prison).

1845- 1901 entries.

1846- 2265 entries

1847-2640 entries

1848- 2533 entries

1849- 1574 entries

1850-1267 entries

The suspect's religion was introduced in Newgate's register in May 1847 for the first time. This is much later than for Kilmainham Jail which started the practice in 1843.

Some analysis was done of place of origin of prisoners at Newgate. For the period January 1 to May 2 1849, there were 700 entries of which 246 (or 35 %)were not born in Dublin at all . A proportion had no address provided so this percentage may have been even larger. Not surprisingly neighbouring counties featured most prominently. But there were more felons born in England than were born in twenty-five out of the thirty two counties of Ireland. (Five out of this twenty-five were deserting soldiers.) Similarly half of the six Scots-born felons were army deserters.

Table 15: Place of Origin of Prisoners at Newgate, Jan 1 to May 2, 1849

Wicklow	27
Kildare	24
Meath	22

England ……………………………………………	21
Offaly ……………………………………………..	12
Tipperary ,Westmeath, Kilkenny, Cork, Wexford……….	11 each
Galway …………………………………………	10
Queens County……………………………….…	9
Cavan, Limerick ………………………………….	7 each
Carlow, Longford, Scotland………………………	6 each
Louth, Mayo…………………………………….	5 each
Roscommon, Leitrim, Kerry, Continental Europe……	4 each
America, Monaghan,Tyrone, Waterford…………….	3 each
Clare, Down…….. …………………………………………	2 each
Newry, Armagh, Sligo…... …………………………	1 each

'Under a Novel Principle' [93]
Mountjoy Jail

The original site for this convict jail was to be the Merrion Road, Black-rock, but this was rejected in favour of its present site as it was locked in by the royal canal and wasn't seen as prone to flooding. [94] Designed by Jacob Owen but based heavily on England's Pentonville Prison, Mountjoy opened in 1850 . Its design reflected the vogue among mid- Nineteenth Century penal thinkers for fostering rehabilitation through industrial work. Cells were designed for one prisoner. Mountjoy was built exclusively for convicts, a term originally used to describe prisoners who were either sentenced to death or transportation for all or part of a sentence. [95]

From its opening, it was subject to certain pressures . Transportation to the Antipodes stopped and then Dublin's Newgate Jail closed. Closure of the Richmond Bridewell in 1887 increased Mountjoy's role in housing petty criminals, which it was never designed for . Female convicts were admitted from 1858 while petty female offenders were admitted after the closure of Grangegorman Lane Prison in 1897. Mountjoy's records make up the largest of all the prison archives, taking up over thirty-five reels of film. However closer examination reveals that

---

[93] H. Hitchens, Inspector-general of Government Prisons, page 44, Inspector of Government Prisons in Ireland annual report, 1850, 1852. Eppi. http://eppi.dippam.ac.uk.

[94] Tim Carey. *Mountjoy - the Story of a Prison*. Collins Press. Page 37.

[95] Ibid, Page 6.

much of the archive relates to the Twentieth Century. In spite of its size and importance, named indexes aren't available for the researcher until 1892 for women and 1894 for men.

The early Mountjoy records display the typical advantages of convict registers over those of non-government prisons. **Next of kin** were almost invariably identified. There was a greater emphasis on recording marital state and number of children. In addition a closer eye was kept on the prisoners' behaviour via **Character Classification Registers** which recorded on-going grades for Industry (I), Schooling (S), and Discipline (D). This makes the government prison record a particularly dense and complex but fascinating source.

As a rule, convicts tended to be moved around various institutions as the designation of a prison changed. This makes the possibility of tracing a convict easier since if the records for one prison didn't survive, a prisoner's file may well turn up in another place. For instance, in 1855 large numbers of invalid prisoners were transferred from Spike Island (no records for that period) to Philipstown (where records exist) because Spike's breezy, exposed climate was deemed unsuitable .[96] Inspector reports recorded a noticeable decrease in the death rate after transfer.

---

[96] *Proquest*. House of Commons Parliamentary Papers Online. http://parlipapers.chadwyck.co.uk. 1856 [2068] Second annual report of the directors of convict prisons in Ireland, for the year ended 31st December, 1855. Accessed December 7, 2010. Institutional subscription required.

Prisons of Strangers
Naas and Athy

Unusually, Kildare divided its county jail between Athy and Naas prisons.[97] The first jail in Athy was housed in the 16th century White's Castle which still overlooks the river in the town. Its conditions were heavily criticized by prison inspectors from the early Nineteenth Century and a new prison was built in 1830, located on the outskirts of the town off the Carlow Road. The governor was Edward Carter. It was downgraded to a bridewell in 1859-60 at the instigation of the Duke of Leinster , and all the prisoners were removed to Naas. A general register for this jail is available on microfilm at the National Archives from 2nd January 1858 to 14th Feb 1860.[98] An earlier register allows research to be done for a starting period of 1848, before the building of the large-scale Curragh military camp in 1855 influenced the registers greatly. [99]

Athy displayed a high standard of record keeping, surpassing many jails of similar importance . Even an index of names was provided, but with the letter 'E' missing. The record is legible throughout. Information on the general register in-cluded: name, crime, religion, trade, county of residence, age, physical descrip-

---

[97] *Google Books. http:// books.google.com/* .George Long. *The Penny cyclopædia of the Society for the Diffusion of Useful .Vol. 3. page 23.* Accessed October 31, 2010.

[98] National Archives, Dublin. MFGS 51/001

[99] Ibid, MFGS 51/ 052-053 .

tion, (often very detailed including terms such as 'stout made' or 'neat made') where and when tried, and sentence. There was also reference to former committals. One glaring omission that would have proved particularly useful for the population of this jail was marital status. The earlier register was taken up mainly with robbery or assault cases involving local people. A total of 661 names were found in this small but important record.

Naas Jail was completed on the Limerick Road in 1833, replacing an earlier jail which had stood in the town since 1796. It was near both the barracks and the courthouse of the town and served as county jail and remand centre. It was closed in 1896 and demolished in 1961. [100]

The Naas jail registers are found on four rolls of microfilm in the National Archives. [101] They cover the years 1859-1881, almost taking over where Athy Jail leaves off, but with the period between November 1871 and April 1875 missing. The records are in good condition, are highly legible and have the advantage of being indexed alphabetically by name at the beginning of each series, although the dates from Jan 1865- June 1867 are indexed from A - C only and entries for 28th June 1867- to 25th Oct. 1871 are without an index. (These index shortcomings are largely cancelled out by recent digitization). Prisoners' names were often cross-referenced with the earlier Athy registers, which is helpful. 'Place of residence' was replaced by the more accurate 'place of birth' on the register during 1865. Because the admission records of Naas Workhouse and Kildare Lock Hospital have not survived, the Nass and Athy prison records take on an added significance.

Naas, along with Athy before it, had its own unique crime - **trespassing on the Curragh Camp.** The usual sentence was a fine of ten shillings or one week in prison. The sentence was invariably served. The main culprits were young women, most of whom were not local. There are multiple entries for the same people. One individual, Bridget Doolan, appeared up to fifty-six times between the years 1856-8. She was 24 in 1859, 5'3', with brown hair, grey eyes and a fair complexion. She came from Moat or Stradbally and was described as a labourer with no education.

---

[100] Co. Kildare Online Electronic History Journal. http://www.kildare.ie/library/ehistory/2011/02/ Taken from the *Leinster Leader,* Aug 5 1961. Cornelius Brosnan . Accessed Nov 5 2010.

[101] National Archives, Dublin, Naas Prison Register, MFGS 51/160-2 & MFGS 51/092.

It is almost certain that many of the inmates in Athy and Naas jail belonged to the group known as the 'Curragh Wrens', described by journalist James Greenwood for the *Pall Mall Gazette* in 1867.[102]

Kildare County Jail, James Greenwood and the 'Curragh Wrens'

Greenwood identified between fifty and sixty women living on the Curragh plane and using the furze for shelter. His articles describe specific events and individuals, possibly disguised with false names. There was a Mary Burns who died in the furze. The ferocious 5'10' amazon, Kate, whom all the others feared. The wren who could write beautifully (the only one with writing skills according to Greenwood.) There was a Miss Clancy and a girl from Arklow. He described a Bridget Flanagan from Dublin. There was four year old Billy Carson, a child of one of the wrens. These names were cross-referenced with the jail registers for 1867 to see if any could be identified.

What Greenwood didn't mention but what is obvious from the prison records was that at least seven of the habitual camp trespassers were not Irish at all, but came from places like Plymouth, Chester, St Albans, Glasgow, Manchester, Liverpool and Coventry. A Mary Burns was, however, located in the record. She was habitually jailed for camp trespassing over many years and had several aliases - Bridget Byrne, Mary Oates and Mary Hurley. In 1866 she was described as 28 years of age, late of Dublin, illiterate, RC, 5'0' with brown hair, grey eyes and a fresh complexion. Her last entry was for March 1867. After that she disappears from the pages, supporting the theory that she was the individual who died in the furze as mentioned in Greenwood's account. Her death didn't appear to have been registered with the GRO under any of her names.

Nobody from Arklow was identified. A possible match was a Mary Jane Turner, from Wicklow, illiterate, RC, 21 , 5' 1¼', charged with trespass on Oct 25th, 1867. Nobody called Bridget Flanagan was found, although a Margaret Clancy was in evidence from Dec 24th 1864, described as illiterate, RC, from Limerick, 20, 4' 10 ½'. No one matched the description of the much -feared 5'10' 'Kate'. A possible match was Ann Brennan, 5'7', RC, Kilkenny, 28 years in 1867. Often brought in on a charge of drunkenness, she may well have been the culprit,

[102] *Nineteenth Century British Newspapers.* (Part 1). Gale. http://find.galegroup.com.
The Pall Mall Gazette (London, England), 'The Wren of the Curragh'. No. 1-4, October 15,16, 17,19, 1867. Accessed December 1, 2010 via subscription site.

her size exaggerated by the other wrens who were under five feet tall in many cases. There was no evidence of Billy Carson's mother.

Eighty-nine habitual Curragh trespassers were identified for 1867, the year of Greenwood's article. Nine of the trespassers could read and write. Twelve of the eighty-nine were Protestant. (13%). There were two cases of infanticide and one of child desertion for that year. The breakdown of place of origin of the followers was a follows:

Table 16: Place of origin of Camp Followers for 1867

Dublin	**10**
Kildare	**10**
Cork	**7**
England	**7**
Tipperary	**6**
Kilkenny	**5**
Offaly	**4**
Wicklow, Westmeath, Galway	**3**
Limerick, Mayo	**2**
Scotland, Glasgow	**1**

One camp trespasser, Eliza Kiff, (born 1845) was almost certainly the daughter of Thomas and Susan Kiff (nee Cockle), agricultural labourers from St Albans, Hertfordshire. [103] In 1861, Kiff, whose surname is strongly associated with Hertfordshire, was living at St Albans with her mother , a widow, who was to remarry later that year.

•••

1859 recorded a total of 486 prisoners in Naas Jail broken down into 260 males and 226 females. But by 1865 there were 346 males and 810 female entries, a unique ratio for a county prison. [104] The Inspector of Prisons re-

---

[103] *Ancestry*. www.Ancestry.co.uk, *1841 & 1851 Census of England.* Accessed June 12 2011. Commercial site.

[104] National Archives, Dublin, Naas Prison Register. 1863-1864. MFGS 51/161.

port for that year reveals that only Cork City jail had a greater preponderance of females[105]. In 1866 the numbers in the jail reached their peak at 1275. There was an increasingly large cohort of male , foreign-born, non-military prisoners in evidence, perhaps reflecting the role of the Curragh in attracting a cosmopolitan mix of craftsmen,tradesmen and musicians. Lombardi, Italy and Baden, Prussia are just some of the places of origin recorded. By October 1870, the word 'Prostitute' was used for the first time to describe some of the camp trespassers. Up until then they were only referred to as 'labourers' or of 'no occupation'. In his book, *A Most Delightful Station*, Con Costello describes the special venom reserved by the local population for the camp followers. [106] The Inspector Reports of the 1860s hint at the reason. Although the army was largely responsible for the influx of these individuals into the area, its compensation system didn't cover this class of prisoner or their offences, and so the considerable cost of their upkeep in jail had to be met by the local rate payers. [107]

There is a break in the Naas records between Oct 25th 1871 and April 28th 1875. But when they resume on 29th April 1875, a great change had occurred. [108] Not only was the number of prisoners greatly reduced (186 in 1876), there were no camp trespassing cases anymore. Instead assault or larceny cases predominated. This may be down to the setting up of a Lock Hospital near Kildare Town in 1869. (Escaping from the Lock had now become a prominent new offence on the register). The **Curragh bye laws** were rewritten in 1873, drastically limiting camp followers to outlying areas. This is likely to be another reason for the major shift in prisoner type. It is also possible that there was an increasing tendency to turn a blind eye to these activities. There were 232 entries up to November 1881 when the register ends abruptly.

Genealogical research of the Naas and Athy prisoners could prove challenging. There is little in the way of familial relationships in this archive. By definition, many of the camp trespassers were cut off from family and community.

[105] Google Books. http:// books.google.com/ . Forty-fifth report of the Inspector-generals of prisons in Ireland for 1866. 1867. X, Accessed December 30 2010.

[106] Con Costello, *A Most Delightful Station*, Collins Press, 1996, page 149, 153

[107] *Proquest*. House of Commons Parliamentary Papers Online. http://parlipapers.chadwyck.co.uk. 1856 [2068 Appendix to Forty-Sixth Report of the Inspector Generals of the General State of Prisons of Ireland for 1867, page 332-3. 1868.

[108] National Archives,Dublin,MFGS 51/092. Naas Prison General Register. 29th April 1875- 21 Nov 1881.

The pattern was for people to feature very prominently for a few years and then to disappear completely. It is difficult to track what happened next . Knowing their ages and various places of origin certainly makes for a solid starting point. If they had children, they were not named by the registers, although offences involving their children identified approximate birth years indirectly. For example - 'Bridget Doolan, 24, from Stradbally, December 1st,1858, was charged with deserting her son, tying him to the workhouse gate and leaving him destitute.' Again on September 25, 1859 she was charged with the same offence. The case was discharged when she herself was sent to the workhouse. With the exception of the English trespassers, these pages are perhaps the best birth record substitutes for the camp followers themselves, many of whom were born in the 1840s and late 1830s.

An example was 'Mary Dixon, born Rathcoole 1840 . 26 years. 5'2'. R.C. Read only. Brown hair and eyes. Sallow skin. Received one month's hard labour for assaulting Colonel Edward Wodehouse, 24th Regiment, 14th June 1866, by throwing stones at him.' There was no trace of her baptism in the relevant parish registers like Rathcoole or Saggart. One of the few remaining veterans of the older registers, Mary Dixon was still in evidence in the final pages, though her description indicates that she had shrunk seven inches to 4'7' in the interim, a small but telling detail that only a prison register could reveal . On 20th April 1881 she was tried at Curragh Sessions for assaulting a policeman. Her death occurred in Naas Workhouse in 1891, where she was described as a spinster and servant by trade.[109]

---

[109] GRO death certificate of Mary Dixon of Rathmore, 1881, Apr-Jun, Vol. 2, Page 670.

The Iron Jail
Philipstown Government Prison

Philipstown, (present-day Daingean)named in honour of Philip of Spain, was the site of assizes and the county jail for King's County in the Eighteenth Century. The jail was located at Snugborough beside an army barracks, but it was at the far end of the town from the courthouse. A report in the 1820s found the jail to be unfit for purpose and a new county jail was planned, favouring Tullamore as an alternative location. In 1831-2 an act was passed transferring assizes to Tullamore , thus downgrading Philipstown to common jail status. (Offaly was also represented by Birr Jail , whose records don't survive.) Philipstown's penal profile rose again when it was selected along with Spike Island as a male convict depot in 1847.

One advantage of convict records is that there was a great deal of moving around of prisoners between the depots and institutions. If the records of one prison are unavailable for a particular period, its prisoners may well be picked up in another place. For instance, large numbers of invalids were transferred from Spike Island to Philipstown in 1855 since Spike's breezy, exposed climate was deemed unsuitable for this class of convict. (190 convicts died there in 1852.)There was a noticeable decrease in the death rate for this class after transfer to Philipstown. These infirm prisoners had previously been transferred from Mountjoy to Spike Island. Francis Hogreve, the governor of Spike Island, assumed office in Philipstown.

Total countrywide returns of convicts for 1855, suggest that a large number of convicts, 300, are being sent to Bermuda, even though transportation had officially ended. The journey would have taken about fifteen days. Labouring jobs at the Royal Navy's dockyard awaited the prisoners there. Some insight into their experiences is provided by the Quarterly Returns of the Hulk Establishments (Series HO11) at the National Archives, Kew. John Mitchell's *Jail Journal* also gives a first-hand account of prisoner life in Bermuda although Mitchell himself was notably exempt from the harsh convict regime.

It is worth noting that 683 men received a free pardon for the year 1855 also, no doubt because of acute lack of space in the penal system. (It was estimated that 1,500 extra places would be needed.)The need for recruits for the Crimean War may also have played a role. This trend is reflected in the Philipstown register where there is a noticeable increase in convicts being discharged by order of the Lord Lieutenant. (See Numbers 554 onwards).

A system of convict classification and good conduct badges were put into operation at Philipstown in November 1855. The governor considered it the best incentive to good behaviour, especially among invalids and juveniles. In 1855 the prisoners themselves were engaged in new building work for the prison including a hospital wing. The resulting structure was known as the 'Iron Jail'. The governor noted a lack of skilled tradesmen such as smiths and carpenters for the works . Surprisingly the commonest ailment among prisoners for that year was scrofulous ulcers. The commonest cause of death was phthisis (18 cases).

Philipstown's records run for the entire duration of its existence as a convict depot - that is from 1849 to 1862, when the prison was wound down due to dwindling numbers. (Most of the invalid inmates were returned to Spike Island at this time.) These records are not microfilmed but the original registers , which are in pristine condition, are available to view in the National Archives. Prisoners come from all parts of the country. The collection consists of three books. Details to be found on each prisoner consist of county of origin, physical description, marital status, number of children, trade, education, religion, conduct in jail, previous convictions, previous character.

There is an interesting list of young men sentenced to penal servitude for sacrilege through the 1850s . Their sentences are heavy - ranging from ten years (John Higgins , 19, Cork, RC,1851 and Patrick Simpson,18, Monaghan, Presbyterian, 1850) to life imprisonment (Michael Regan, 21, RC, Cork, 1857.) This particular crime is unusual in that protestants and catholics are equally represented.

In 1855, Philipstown was selected along with Mountjoy Jail for juvenile convicts, until such time as the designated Juvenile Reformatory at Lusk , Dublin, was completed. [110] (Under the subsequent Crofton reform measures, Lusk became an Intermediate Prison instead.)The register records children as young as eleven (prison numbers 751-797.) Most were in prison for robbery and , with a few exceptions, had previous form.

Sometimes the registrar can't resist venting his personal feelings.

'Michael Regan, 17, Tipperary, 7 years for larceny, April 7 1853, RC, R&W, labourer, committed at Newgate Dec 11 1854, disposed of at Mountjoy July 5 1855, incorrigible at Newgate, "badly in want of a flogging".'

Details about prison transfers make tracing and cross checking records of other prisons possible. There is also more emphasis on recording next of kin and number of children in these records.

Perhaps because of its heritage as a centre for juvenile delinquents , a reformatory for boys run by the Oblate Fathers was opened in 1870 near the Philipstown jail and barrack complex.

---

[110] EPPI, *http://eppi.dippam.ac.uk,* Directors of Convict Prisons in Ireland: second annual report, 1855, page 3. Accessed June 30, 2013.

The Criminalizing of Lunatics

Throughout the 1840s and early 1850s a large number of prisoners described as "dangerous lunatics" appeared in the registers of county jails. (They were never detained in bridewells). How did this situation come about? The **Richmond Lunatic Asylum** opened at Grange Gorman, Dublin in 1815 , becoming the first (and also the largest) district asylum in the country under an 1810 Act of Parliament. The Dublin House of Industry (where St James's Hospital is now located) was financed by parliament and contained lunatics from all parts of Ireland. Parliamentary reform giving powers to the Lord Lieutenant to establish provincial asylums was never acted on.   Instead the penal system was used to deal with the mental health problem of Ireland in subsequent decades. Although it may have been difficult to calculate, the 1851 Census of Ireland Report put the number of lunatics in the country at 9980, of whom 4635 were described as being "at large".

On one day, January 1st 1857, 166 lunatics were listed as being imprisoned in jails throughout the country. Of this group only 10 were classed as criminal lunatics. 149 were described as "dangerous lunatics" who had been committed to jail by the process of two Justices for the Peace under *1 Vic.,c.27*; and *8&9 Vic.,c. 107,sec.10*. These individuals had not committed any crime but had been apprehended under some derangement of mind and under circumstances where some crime might be intended. In this way the insane entered the criminal system. In effect, the only way lunatics could access an asylum was through the prison system and in this way they or their families were forced to interact with the criminal system.

There was some suspicion expressed by officials at the time that families were using the Dangerous Lunatics Acts to shift the burden of their relative's upkeep onto the state. The report of 1857 found that jails were entirely unsuitable places for the insane and strongly recommended a change in the law to allow a justice to commit someone directly to a district asylum, as was the case in England. The necessary legislation for doing this wasn't enacted until 1867, however. Even then , some justices ignored the new system. There were sixteen district asylums in 1857, a number that was considered wholly inadequate. This meant that lunatics spent more time in jail than was intended: in one case up to eight years.

Dundrum Asylum was opened in 1850 and catered for those indicted or acquitted of a crime by virtue of insanity. But as space was inadequate the authorities had to be selective. Those guilty of a heinous crime were given first priority. But if behaviour was disturbed and crime was small, this group could end up in Dundrum also. It would perhaps seem more appropriate that Dundrum's records should fall under the ambit of prison registers . But at the time of printing, there are no plans to make its records available to the public. Thus the Richmond Asylum records, dealt with in the chapter on Grangegorman Lane Prison, are unique in terms of freedom of access. With the proposed development of the Grangegorman site by Dublin Institute of Technology, a society has been established to create an on-site museum where the asylum records which date from 1814 will be available for public research. [111]

---

[111] Grangegorman Community Museum, http://www.grangegorman.ie Accessed July 2013.

'The Most Disturbed District' [112]
The Two Jails of Tipperary

As the administrative capital of the sprawling county of Tipperary, Clonmel was the location for the county jail. The wars between the Butlers and Desmonds in the 16th Century and the Cromwellian occupation of the town in the 17th ensured that the county's penal tradition would be long and significant. [113] Tipperary was always a hot bed of agrarian unrest, earning Viscount Melbourne's description as 'the most disturbed district' in the 1830s, then going on to become one of the districts covered by the Crime and Outrage in Ireland Bill of 1847 . Regretfully, its records from the 1820s and 30s don't survive , leaving Cork County Jail as perhaps the best record for Whiteboy activity from a penal viewpoint.

Built at Richmond (now Emmett) Street in 1834 beside an older jail which dated from 1790, Clonmel remained the county jail for all of Tipperary until Nenagh prison was completed in 1842. After this time it served the South Riding of Tipperary only. Clonmel had a separate prison and hospital for men and women, a free-standing marshalsea , a school and a chapel. By the 1840s it had begun two unusual and profitable businesses - taking in laundry for Clonmel families and cleaning the dormitories of the local army barracks. [114] It was closed in

---

[112] John Henry Barrow, Ed., *The Mirror of Parliament. Debates, Proceedings Etc. of the Imperial Parliament of Great Britain and Ireland*, 1837-8, Volume 1, page 174, London. (Viscount Melbourne describing County Tipperary in the House of Lords, Nov. 27, 1837.)

[113] Michael Ahern, *Clonmel County Gaol*, pages 1-2. Ardo Books. 2010.

[114] Michael Ahern,*Clonmel County Gaol,* page 27

August 1910 to make way for a borstal. Surviving archival records run from 1840 to 1928, so taking in eighteen years of its time as a borstal. The original registers are available over five microfilms in the National Archives on a self-service basis and are also searchable by name on the *Familysearch* website. They are in good condition throughout and there is no evidence of water damage or deterioration.

An unusual feature is that the early records, from June 19, 1840 to April 8, 1842, then from March 12, 1845 - Feb 26, 1848 , consist of **assizes notebooks** with hand-ruled columns and margins on a plain ledger. [115](Assizes were held in the local courthouse.) In the earlier ledger, details on the defendants include name, age, religion, date and how disposed of and whether the defendant can read or write. There is a separate column recording which Riding the offender is from - denoted by an "N" or an "S". (Tipperary's division into two Ridings dates from December 1838) [116]. The second ledger , 1845-1848, is more detailed and includes defendant's number of previous visits to jail and colour of eyes, hair and complexion. These details are early by county jail standards. Recording of education is dropped from March 1845 onwards, however, and is not resumed until 1848. Through these years the columns are bitty and untidy and look like they've been hastily ruled in by the clerk, although the information is still legible.

There is a general register for the prison on proper headed note paper spanning the years September 30, 1841 to June 26, 1845, duplicating much of the assize notebooks. They are very neat with numbered entries but are a step down from the assize journals in terms of prisoner detail provided. For instance no religion or Riding is recorded .

There appear to be a great deal of rioting cases through the 1840s in this area. They frequently involve fathers and sons. An example of one riot on July 5th 1844 involving twenty-nine individuals included seven members of an extended family:

Michael Breen. 23 (write)
Michael Breen Jnr. 20 (alphabet)
Thomas Breen Jnr. 26 (write)
Thomas Breen the 3RD . 23 (write)
William Breen .21 (read)

---

[115] National Archives , MFGS 51/004. Clonmel Gaol Registers June 1840- Feb 1848.

[116] Michael Ahern, *Clonmel Gaol*, page 32

John Breen. 23 (write)

Thomas Breen. 30 (write)

Frustratingly, at the end of 1844, the registrar stops filling in age and education in respect of rioting and rescue cases. (Other classes are kept as they are). The same fate befalls vagrancy cases from 1850 onwards.

Clonmel was a garrison town since 1780 and by 1841 had a thriving population of 13,000. [117] A large number of cases involving soldiers who have breached the "articles of war" are evident from the beginning in the records. The usual sentence is forty days hard labour and confinement.

In the early 1840s the Clonmel area was characterized by a lot of court cases involving cutting whitethorn, blackthorn, underwood or furze . This activity carried a sentence of between fourteen days to one month hard labour. There were also many cases of trespassing on the mountain of either Lord Lismore or Lord Glengall (Richard Butler) on the part of large groups of young people who appear not to be related. Rioting and breaches of the peace involved a lot of family members. For instance, three brothers , James 23, John, 25 and William, 20, Connors , no education, were bailed and discharged for such an offence in May 7, 1842. There is also an interesting murder case involving members of the same family.

Philip Ryan 49

John Ryan 38

Michael Ryan 17

Bridget Ryan 48

Mary Ryan 17

Nancy Ryan 20

Patrick Ryan 12

For murder of Michael Ryan, April 6 1843. The first three were confined for between 7-9 months with hard labour. The remainder were discharged.

Clonmel adopts a new register format in 1848 with designated columns for height and physical description. [118] Disappointingly,many of the vagrant prisoners don't have any of their details filled in other than their name.

---

[117] Cormac O'Grada, *Ir. Econ. Soc. Hist. XVIII* (1991) , 24-33. "The Heights of Clonmel Prisoners 1845-9: some dietary implications". Page 25.

[118] National Archives, MFGS 51/092.

Clonmel's register of male and female Juveniles from 1862-1878 demonstrates how different these records are from the normal format.[119] They record whether a child or his parents were in the workhouse, whether his parents had been in jail, whether one, both or no parents were living,whether the child was illegitimate or a step child. There are 490 children under sixteen in this database with a number of brothers in evidence.

The other major jail in Tipperary, Nenagh, was upgraded from a bridewell to the county jail for Tipperary North Riding in 1842. It was located beside the court house where the holding of assizes was granted under an act of parliament in 1838. The Gate house and Governor's house are now a heritage centre.

The jail to which these surviving records relate was completed in 1843. It consisted of 192 cells, 20 day and work rooms, 11 yards, 52 individual cells, a chapel, treadwheel, kitchen, laundry. There was no heating throughout the building. There was no school either initially but the governor, a Mr Smyth, saw to it at once. Nenagh Jail's structure allowed for four prisoner classifications, and the separation of male and female. Standard of officials was deemed good in prison reports. [120]

Inevitably it is tempting to make a comparison between the records of Clonmel and Nenagh. When Clonmel adopted a new register format in 1848, this put it well ahead of several comparable county jails but well behind its sister jail of Nenagh which included these features from as early as March 1843. In addition to being neater, Nenagh's records also offer the researcher more variety because its Debtors' Register has survived for the years 1843-1872. One drawback of the Nenagh records is that they are missing for most of the 1850s and stop in 1884, much earlier than Clonmel. Both jails archives are without a surviving index.

---

[119] National Archives. MFGS 51/008.

[120] Proquest. House of Commons Parliamentary Papers Online. http://parlipapers.chadwyck.co.uk .1844 [535] Prisons of Ireland. Twenty-second report of the inspectors-general on the general state of the prisons of Ireland, 1843: with appendices. Page 94.Accessed January 3rd 2011.

Complementary Records

Inspector Reports

It is well worth studying the prison registers in conjunction with the yearly Inspector-General of Prisons reports prepared for the House of Commons since 1822 and , from 1879, the reports of the General Prisons Board. These official documents are available in hardcopy at the British Library and on the internet through the *Proquest* site, where they are digitised and fully searchable. To a certain extent they can fill the vacuum created by the destruction of important prison archives like, for example, Mullingar and Lifford. They allow the researcher to find out the size of the archive they are dealing with by providing annual population returns for each jail. Statistics on fluctuating numbers, rate of reoffending and type of crime on the wane or the increase are also available. An example is provided below.

	1847.	1848.	Increase.	Decrease.
Treason,	–	8	8	–
Felons,	631	496	–	135
Larceny,	709	1,067	358	–
Misdemeanants,	1,866	2,054	188	–
Revenue Laws,	9	24	15	–
Poor Laws.	11	13	2	–
Court-martial,	–	223	223	–
Vagrants,	535	1,833	1,298	–
Drunkards,	1,447	1,621	174	–
Lunatics,	71	44	–	27
Total,	5,279	7,383	2,104	–
Daily Average,	262	346	84	–
Highest Number,	403	433	30	–
Lowest Number,	201	211	10	–
Average in Hospital,	24	19	–	5
Deaths,	25	16	–	9

Periods of Imprisonment in 1848.

	Felons and Misdemeanants.	Vagrants.	Drunkards.		Felons and Misdemeanants.	Vagrants.	Drunkards.
2 Years,	6	–	–	14 Days,	554	6	–
18 Months,	2	–	–	7 Days,	645	1,080	–
12 Months,	64	–	–	3 Days,	–	22	–
9 Months,	7	–	–	2 Days (48 hours),	435	–	58
6 Months,	148	–	–	1 Day (24 hours),	519	708	1,563
3 Months,	376	–	–	Unlimited,	63	–	–
2 Months,	434	–	–				
1 Month,	676	17	–		3,929	1,833	1,621

Of this list of felons and misdemeanants—

Read and write,			1,919
Read only,			261
Illiterate,			1,749
Total,			3,929

And of the vagrant list were—

Natives of Dublin,			285
Natives of other counties,			1,548
Total,			1,833

Table 17: Richmond Bridewell derived from Inspector General's Report comparing 1847 and 1848. [121] *Numbers of vagrants coming from outside of Dublin is revealing.*

---

[121] *Proquest.* House of Commons Parliamentary Papers Online. http://parlipapers.chadwyck.co.uk. 1849 [1069] Prisons of Ireland. Twenty-seventh report of the Inspectors-General on the general state of the prisons of Ireland, 1848; with appendices. Page 31. Accessed Mar 1 2011. Institutional subscription required.

A report from 1837 provides all the names of convicts discharged before their sentences expired. [122] (Appendix G starting on page 1388). The list consists of 2153 names. With a total of 136, convicts from County Tipperary secured the most pardons. Prisons whose records have not survived, such as Donegal, Drogheda, Omagh, Londonderry, and Monaghan are included in this list. The next appendix deals with prisoners whose sentences were commuted since may 1st 1835. This consists of 2513 names. Again Tipperary jail has the most cases at 193. In the case of Sligo - many of the cases are breaches of the excise laws. Appendix K reproduces the sixteen favourable prisoners' memorials to the Lord Lieutenant, Lord Mulgrave Constantine Phipps, on foot of his tour of prisons in August 1836. Many of the reports contain details of prisoners in the course of an official investigation. An example of this was the inquest in 1862 into the death of Alice Delin, a 79 year old dealer who had lived for forty years in Killelaney Geashill, and who died after spending seven days at Tullamore Jail. Tullamore prison registers for females do not survive for the year covered in this report, so the report itself is a useful substitute. It names Elizabeth Dillin, Newtown,servant, as the victim's daughter and informant. (The report was highly critical of Thomas Weldon Trench, the justice for the county who made a citizen's arrest of Delin under *Vic 10 & 11 Vict. C 84.* [123]) A better example from a genealogical point of view is the case of Archibald Slyne, indicted for the murder of Reverend John Walshe, Carlow,in 1838. Detailed information is provided about the many family members of the witnesses, the Rooneys and the Hawleys. [124]

The inspector reports are also a good source of information on the identities of the many staff who manned these prisons - often a neglected aspect of genealogical research. An example is the 1842 report listing all 70 officers working

[122] Ibid, (194) Convicts (Ireland). Return of the names of convicts discharged from the several gaols in Ireland, before the expiration of their sentences, since 1st May 1835, &c.). Accessed December 12 , 2010.

[123] *Ibid,* 1862 (377) Alice Delin. Copies of the depositions taken at a coroner's inquest held at Tullamore. Accessed December 10 2010.

[124] *Ibid,* 1839 (486) Report from the Select Committee of the House of Lords, appointed to enquire into the state of Ireland in respect of crime. Page 1391. Accessed November 1 2010 .

at Newgate Jail, Dublin.[125]The inspectors-general were dependent on locally appointed supervisors for their information, which may have led to a certain bias or
inaccuracy .[126] For this reason it can be useful to compare totals in the original
registers with what appeared in the reports.

The reports are a useful window into the mindset of Victorian prison administrators who quote the works of European penologists like Thomas Berenger
(1785 -1866) and Franz von Holtzendorff (1829-1889). Firm advocates of complete separation of prisoners in preference to a regime of silence , both Europeans
were cited in these reports and it would appear that the authorities were aiming to
implement their theories in the prisons under their jurisdiction.[127]

Prison Correspondence

This collection takes up an entire wall of the National Archives in Dublin
and represents a treasure trove. The collection starts in 1850 and runs up to 1924-
25 (GPO up to 1878. GPB from 1879. 141 volumes). Each year comes with an
index . Northern Irish prisons and prisons whose archives don't survive such as
Drogheda and Lusk are included in the archive. Alphabetically arranged by subject , writer's name and prison, this collection is probably the best source of information about **prison employees**. It also has extensive lists under headings such
as sick prisoners, memorialists, insanity cases, prisoners assisted with emigration,
Presbyterian inmates, qualifications and gratuities of warders.

For example , the margin of Castlebar Jail's general register referred to
correspondence about a prisoner, James Morley. 24. Lauralea, Aghamor, Bally-
haunis, in the 'letter book'. Page and date of entry was provided. 'Entered Ulster
Bank with intent to commit felony' October 30th, 1896. Sent to Galway for trial
1896. A reference is made to Galway winter assizes, December 2, 1896. Found

---

[125] *Ibid,* Inspector General Report of Prisons of Ireland, 1842. Page 19. Accessed Dec 1st 2010 .
Institutional Subscription required.

[126] Beverly A. Smith, 'The Female Prisoner in Ireland 1855-1878'. *Federal Probation, Vol. 54,
Issue 4*(Dec 1990), page 71.

[127] *Proquest. House of Commons Parliamentary Papers Online.*
http://parlipapers.chadwyck.co.uk. 1867-8. Forty-sixth report of the inspectors-general on the
general state of the prisons of Ireland, 1867, page 316. Accessed May 2nd 2011. Institutional Subscription Required.

insane by jury. Sent to Dundrum Asylum December 10, 1896. A search of the Correspondence Book for 1896 reveals the existence of a letter from his solicitor as to his sanity and a medical report. [128] The correspondence register, arranged by number, contains a precis of the letter's contents.

Convict Reference Files

Convicts were entitled to appeal to the Viceroy for commutation or remission of their sentence once a year. It was an expensive exercise for most as it involved paying a lawyer to frame the petition in rather formal, ingratiating terms. [129] Cases were handled by the Convict Department of the Chief Secretary's Office. The archive is divided into two sections which are now microfilmed. The first deals with petitions from prisoners and next of kin starting in 1787.[130] It is arranged chronologically, though there is an alphabetically arranged card index of names of convicts available from 1796-1835 for ease of reference. The memorials are copied in negative form and the oldest ones are difficult to read. These documents are particularly significant since convicts records before 1836 were destroyed in the Four Courts fire of 1922 and the petitions(plus of course any surviving prison records) are the only remaining evidence. The second section in the series is larger and deals with petitions relevant to the main Australian transportation years of 1835-1856. It is chronological and arranged loosely by surname. It too is available in the National Archives. [131] A selective database of 38,907 convicts spanning the entire transportation era is searchable by name on the National Archive's website[132] and provides a reference number to pinpoint the original documents .

The use of such memorials in genealogy is well illustrated by the example of Robert Robinson in 1839. [133]

---

[128] National Archives, Dublin. CGB,CR,74. 13466,13559,13719.

[129] Tim Carey, *Mountjoy - the Story of a Prison.* Page 132. Collins Press 2000.

[130] National Archives, Dublin, CSO, CD, Prisoners' Petitions and Cases, MFS 57/1-14

[131] Ibid, CSO, CD,CRF, MFS 59/1-77

[132] *The National Archives of Ireland.* Ireland-Australia transportation database. http://www.nationalarchives.ie.Accessed February 12 ,2011.

[133] National Archives of Ireland. MFS 59/14. CRF 1839 R45.

Case history from Convict Reference Files

Robert Robinson faced seven years transportation for bigamy. The memorial is written by his sister, Mrs Captain Elizabeth Murray of Sandymount. She cites that their uncle, Edward Andrew Robinson, was a magistrate in Queen's County who died in 1812, leaving a large fortune. That Robinson had married Ellen Porter, a 'low character', in 1825 without knowledge or consent of his family. He was 23 years of age at the time. There is reference also to a marriage settlement with a George Bingham, staffman to Lord Mayor, named as trustee. Robinson was said to have several brothers older than himself, three in Queen's County, one a Captain in the East India Company. After leaving his wife in 1828, he married Miss Elizabeth Eaton of Maryborough, also without knowledge of his family. His second wife, Elizabeth Eaton, also provided a memorial on Robinson's behalf, stating she was the daughter of Benjamin Eaton, builder and architect, Dublin. She was expecting a child in a few months, and stated that her own foolishness in not making more enquiries was a major factor in the debacle.

Convict Reference Books 1836-1922, (CON CRB)

This is a sixteen volume collection of original ledgers situated on the open shelves of the National Archives, Dublin. It can be a useful finding aid as names are alphabetically arranged by year, (usually the year of the prisoner's release). The information available includes name of prisoner, county of origin, whether transported, imprisoned fined or died. If a petition for clemency was sent to the Lord Lieutenant the book will indicate whether the outcome was favourable or not, and will give details of level of sentence on appeal.

General Prisons Board Penal Records

This is a collection of detailed case files on prisoners dating from just before the time of the GPB's foundation in 1879. A detailed dossier for each prisoner gives information on age, health, occupation, diet, correspondence and visits (invariably family members, if at all), conduct in prison and punishments incurred. Then from 1889 photographs of the convict were taken at the start and end of the sentence. This allows the researcher to compare the before and after appearance, which is often quite shocking.

A draft finding aid for this collection is now available on the open shelf for 1877-1926 under the GPB/PEN series. (Since January 2011 to date this book has been withdrawn from the open shelf and has to be asked for at the counter.) Arranged by release year and reference number, names are listed in most cases. There are several hundred names in this list. The Convict Reference Books (above) can supply the prisoner's release year, which is vital for using this series.

The Challenge of Aliases

This is a particular issue with both perpetual female and juvenile offenders. A typical page of entries at Grangegorman jail for 1880 reveals that of the twenty-two women on the page, sixteen had aliases. Six had three or more, five had two or more.[134] This was not untypical. Luckily, the prison authorities approached the alias problem by laboriously listing every name that a prisoner had been known to use in the past with each entry. If the prisoner was given a lengthy sentence a single name was usually decided on which was presumably considered the most authentic.

Some cases were plainly a play on a name, such as Hannon becoming Hanlon or Hand. Another reason for aliases was clearly an attempt by a prisoner with a distinctive name to stick out less, as with Augustus Achilles (25 years), shoemaker, RC, born Meeting house Yard, adopting the name of Frederick Flanagan at the Richmond Bridewell in 1865.

The case of recidivist juveniles was equally bad. One of the more extreme cases was that of Pat Cosgrave, a thief since the age of eight .'Committed to Richmond Bridewell 14th Jan. 1852. 13 years old. (4'3 ¾'.) Brown hair. Fresh complexion. Born Watling Street. R.C. No education. Loitering to commit felony. Two months' [135]. His creative collection of aliases included Edward Kisby. James

---

[134] National Archives. Gen. Register Grangegorman Women's Prison. MFGS 51/ 041. Page 1140.

[135] Ibid, MFGS 51/067.

Duff. Richard Kisby. Maddock, Murphy, Gilmore, Halloran and Flynn. Might they be a clue to a mother's surname or wider family?

Further enquiries established that this prisoner was sentenced to seven years transportation in 1852 under the name Edward Kisby, for felony of a hand-kerchief. He was sent to Spike Island instead and then on to Phillipstown in 1854. [136] Unusually, Philipstown gave no information about next of kin as they usually did and so it is possible he may not have had any . He received schooling while at Phillipstown and very likely a trade, earning a first class badge under the Crofton System. [137] Like many convicts, he was released by the Lord Lieutenant in 1856 due to lack of prison space. The GRO lists an Edward Kisby, shoemaker, New-town Park Avenue, Blackrock Dublin , marrying a Mary Kelly or Kennedy , servant , in 1871.[138] His father was named as Edward Kisby, deceased.

---

[136] Phillipstown Register of Convicts Book. GPO/PN 3. Number 754.

[137] Philipstown Convict Character Book. GPO/PN 5. Number 754.

[138] GRO Marriage of Edward Kisby 1871 , Vol 7, page 876.

Conclusion

At their best, prison registers are possibly the most detailed database of names, addresses and occupations of a surprisingly broad cross-section of Irish society - reflecting the twin Victorian traits of zealous record-keeping and zero tolerance to crime. As such they more than complement Griffith's *Valuation* and other Irish 19th Century census substitutes, particularly for the era before Civil Registration, while providing the researcher with that extra layer of insight through detailed physical descriptions and religion . In this sense they are more comprehensive than English penal records which do not routinely supply either religion or physical description of the prisoner. They offer a variety of uses for the data they hold and also come with an impressive set of complementary records. Among these uses would include surname analysis, study of demography and population migration, census and birth record substitutes, study of addresses in relation to crime (particularly useful for Dublin), and more specific studies like height analysis or the incidence of scarring and physical defect in the prison population.

Though it was by no means the case that crime was found to run in families, nonetheless certain offences had a strong familial dimension to them. This is illustrated by Table 18 below .

Table 18: Most Familial Offences

Offence	Locations	Observations
Faction Fighting/ Rioting	Common in midland jails such as Maryborough, Clonmel and Nenagh, 1830s and 1840s	Large numbers of people brought in. Prisoner details often left out however
Begging/Vagrancy	Widespread and involving whole families during Famine years. Otherwise mainly in city jails	Poor survival rate of specific records
Rescue	County jails	Springing of defendants or arrestees from police custody by groups of relations
Illicit Distilling	Sligo	Young and old, male and female. Location of still often identified
Assault	Widespread	Involving male members of same family, often over several generations.

Findings indicated that debtors were often the exception to the rule statistically, being the stand-out prison population in several surveys undertaken. The prison service's diligence in recording religious profession, long before the 1861 Census and its reports did so, allows statistical data to be collected on this subject for quite a large section of a community. Every jail has something unique to offer the researcher and tells a revealing story about a local area. A perfect example of this is Naas Jail and the Curragh Camp trespassers. Sligo Jail proved to be the most useful archive for its size, given the variety, detail and early starting date of its registers and its role in enhancing the Mayo Traveller survey.

A disadvantage of this type of source is that searches for relations are often speculative and time-consuming due to the lack of widespread indexes, although this has been solved by recent digitization programmes. [139] However indexes were found to be more plentiful than first thought, particularly for the Famine years where record-keeping would be expected to be most chaotic. The survey found a huge variation in record-keeping standards between county and in some cases government jails of comparable size and status, in spite of obvious attempts by central governing bodies to standardize them. 1848 and 1878 proved to be watershed years in the registers. In spite of the slight increase in prison numbers in 1878-79, the overall trend was firmly downwards, leaving the authorities confident to close many county jails and bridewells in this period. Table 19 below shows the decline. As a result Prison Registers become a less valuable archive for the historian and genealogist from this time on.

---

[139] familysearch.org, Accessed July 2013.

No. 1.—NUMBER OF PRISONERS (of all Classes) IN COUNTY AND BOROUGH GAOLS on the 1st January in each year.							Numbers in custody on the 1st January in each of the last 30 years.
On 1st January, 1851,	.	10,084	On 1st January, 1866,	.	2,663		
Do. do. 1852,	.	8,803	Do. do. 1867,	.	2,332		
Do. do. 1853,	.	7,604	Do. do. 1868,	.	2,463		
Do. do. 1854,	.	5,755	Do. do. 1869,	.	2,024		
Do. do. 1855,	.	5,080	Do. do. 1870,	.	2,029		
Do. do. 1856,	.	3,561	Do. do. 1871,	.	2,161		
Do. do. 1857,	.	3,419	Do. do. 1872,	.	2,098		
Do. do. 1858,	.	3,265	Do. do. 1873,	.	2,477		
Do. do. 1859,	.	2,844	Do. do. 1874,	.	2,609		
Do. do. 1860,	.	2,535	Do. do. 1875,	.	2,517		
Do. do. 1861,	.	2,488	Do. do. 1876,	.	2,498		
Do. do. 1862,	.	2,916	Do. do. 1877,	.	2,229		
Do. do. 1863,	.	3,055	Do. do. 1878,	.	2,817		
Do. do. 1864,	.	3,023	Do. do. 1879,	.	2,497		
Do. do. 1865,	.	2,747	Do do. 1880,	.	2,690		

Table 19: taken from the Second Report of the GPB to Parliament ,1880, page 9.

The list below records some of the various groups found in the registers, reinforcing the theory that prison populations were particularly representative of the population at large, perhaps more so than other key records. In this sense they are on a par with petty session records but the latter rarely give the same level of detail on a defendant.

Children - found frequently in county jails until 1859.

Women - often a third of the population on the register.

First time offenders - the O'Grada study of Clonmel Prison (1845- 49) f o u n d that for most in the register it was their first brush with the law.[140]

Army deserters- often English or Scottish.

Occupational offenders - Can be broadly divided into two main categories. Car drivers who kill or maim pedestrians and those who abscond from work apprenticeships without permission. One aspect of 19th century Dublin prison records that stands out is the large numbers of cab drivers sent up on manslaughter

---

[140] Research_Online@UCD, Cormac O'Grada. 'Heights in Tipperary in the 1840s : evidence from prison
registers'. *Ir. Econ. Soc. Hist. XVIII(1991)*, page 25. Accessed June 20th 2011.

charges due to fatal collisions. Judgements tended to be lenient and most of those committed got off.

Users of profane language - In 1899, 18% of female offenders on the general register of Mountjoy jail were there for this offence. (usual sentence was 7 days). [141]

Felons and convicts

Debtors- 8-12% of county prison population.

Drunk and disorderlies

Vagrants

Lunatics - a sizable proportion in county jails.

Customs and Excise offenders (see Sligo Jail).

Faction Fighters. [142] The statement of Inspector General in the RIC, Colonel James Shaw Kennedy, on the state of crime in Ireland, 1839, commissioned for the House of Lords described faction fighting as follows:

> *Fights which took place in Ireland in consequence of the Quarrels arising from local Circumstances, and Quarrels of Families, increased by one Family joining another and taking the Part of another; the local Quarrels of Ireland; and those Quarrels were decided at Fairs and Markets by Combats.*

Train fare dodgers- The first Irish commuter rail route, Dublin to Kingstown, was opened in 1836 .The Great Southern and Western Railway followed in 1846. Dublin to Drogheda line was reached in 1844. This transport revolution marked a subtle change in the nature of prison records. From the early 1850s a steady trickle of offences connected in various ways with the railway become a regular feature of the registers. These included children putting stones on the railway track, passengers dodging fares, individuals trespassing on the tracks, passengers travelling in the wrong class of carriage (there were four in the early days). Whole families were brought in in some instances. In her book , *Every Dark Hour* , Niamh O'Sullivan cites the example of three members of the Lyons family, Alan (36), Ann (27) and Catherine (5) all from Scotland, who were sentenced to a week in Kilmain-

---

[141] National Archives, Dublin, General Register of Female Prisoners Mountjoy Jail ,MFGS 51/067.

[142] Proquest .House of Commons Parliamentary Papers Online. 2006.
http://parlipapers.chadwyck.co.uk. 1839(486) Report from the Select Committee of the House of Lords, appointed to enquire into the state of Ireland in respect of crime,and to report theron to the house ; page 434. Accessed January 8, 2011.

ham in 1855 for having no ticket.[143]   Further enquiry at the comprehensive Scot-landspeople website failed to locate any member of this family , and it's possible that they gave aliases to the jail authorities. This category of misdemeanour is supplemented by tram fare dodging in later years .

Penalties can be quite heavy , as if the authorities mean to make an example of the culprits. On April 15, 1854, a group of young friends, including two sisters, were jailed at Kilmainham for two months with hard labour for having a stolen railway ticket in their possession.

Anne Cooney, 13, Dublin
Alice Cooney, 19, Kingstown
Honour Bond, 17, Kingstown
Mary Gamel, 18, Limerick.

Then on May 9 1854, Edward Holly , 11, Patrick Hanaway, 10, and Michael Farrell, 15, all from Tipperary, were jailed for 14 days in lieu of a fine of 6/11 for travelling the line without tickets.

October 20, 1854, John Murray (40) , RC, 5'7", hazel eyes, grey eyes, swarthy complexion, twenty-four hours or a five shilling fine for trespassing on the Great Southern or Western Railway.

Cruelty to animal offenders
Quite numerous in Carrick on Shannon prison records where a five shilling fine or one week in prison was the normal penalty. [144]

Sacrilege offenders. Invariably young men with an even split between Catholic and Protestant offenders. (See Philipstown Jail records.)

---

[143] Niamh O'Sullivan, *Every Dark Hour : a History of Kilmainham Jail*. Page 203-4.

[144] National Archives, Dublin, MFGS 51/002.

Those in breach of firearm regulations

In 1847, parliament introduced the Prevention of Crime and Outrage in Ireland Bill . [145] The act placed constraints including penalties for keeping unregistered firearms on certain districts deemed to be turbulent. Prosecutions for keeping a firearm illegally were especially noticeable in Queen's County prison records. [146] The penalty was up to one month in jail.

---

[145] Fiona Slevin, *By hereditary virtues: a history of Lough Rynn,* page 109. Coolabawn Publishing, 2006.

[146] National Archives, Dublin, MFGS 51/145.

Figure (i) Entrance to St Michan's Park , Dublin, showing the outline of the old turreted corner of Newgate Gaol

Figure (ii) Facade of Grangegorman Lane Women's Prison, Grangegorman, Dublin

Figure (iii) Main entrance of Richmond Bridewell Prison, South Circular Road, Dublin

Appendix 1. Available Jail Registers at National Archives of Ireland

Athy

Record Type	Dates Covered	Reference No.
General Register	Aug 5 1848- Dec 30 1855	MFGS 51/ 052-53
General Register	Jan 1858- Feb 14 1860	MFGS 51/001

Carrick on Shannon

Record Type	Dates Covered	Reference No.
General Register	Aug 1849- Oct 1855	MFGS 51/002
General Register	Jan 29 1869- Dec 19 1878	MFGS 51/002
General Register	Jan 2 1879- Mar 27 1880	MFGS 51/002
Quarterly Returns of Prisoners	Jun 30 1880 - Mar 31 1891	MFGS 51/002
Quarterly Returns of Prisoners	Jun 30 1891 - Dec 31 1901	MFGS 51/002-003

Clonmel

Record Type	Dates Covered	Reference No.
Assizes Journals	Jun 19 1840- Apr 8 1842. Mar 12 1845- Feb 26 1848	MFGS 51/ 004
General Register	Sep 30 1841- Jun 26 1845	MFGS 51/ 004 -5
General Register	Jun 26 1848 - Dec 14 1852	MFGS 51/ 005-6
General Register	Jan 1 1857- Sep 23 1878	MFGS 51/ 006 -7
General Register	Oct 2 1878- Dec 30 1880	MFGS 51/ 007
General Register	Mar 29 1883 - Dec 31 1893	MFGS 51/ 007
General Register	Jan 1 1894- Jan 28 1903	MFGS 51/ 007
Register of male and female juveniles (16 and under)	Jan 11 1862 - Sep 11 1878	MFGS 51/ 008

Cork City Jail

Record Type	Dates Covered	Reference No.
Register of Convicted Prisoners	Aug 23 1823- Dec 31 1844	MFGS 51/010-11
Register of Convicted Prisoners	Dec 16 1848- Dec 14 1850	MFGS 51/010-11
Register of Convicted Prisoners	Jan 2 1860- Apr 30 1864	MFGS 51/011
Register of Convicted Prisoners	Oct 7 1870- Mar 30 1878	MFGS 51/011-12

Cork County Jail

Record Type	Dates Covered	Reference No.
Register of Convicted Prisoners	Aug 23 1823- Dec 31 1844	MFGS 51/010-11
House of Correction Journal	May 27 1824- Dec 31 1837	MFGS 51/023
Register of Prisoners Committed from Petty Sessions	Oct 7 1847- Oct 17 1849	MFGS 51/024-25
Ledger on Court Decisions (petty to serious)	Jun 16 1830- May 21 1834	MFGS 51/013
Ledger on Court Decisions	May 27 1834- Apr 9 1839	MFGS 51/014

Record Type	Dates Covered	Reference No.
Ledger on Court Decisions	Mar 20 1847- Jun 7 1848	MFGS 51/014
Ledger on Court Decisions	Mar 24 1850- Mar 7 1852	MFGS 51/014
General Register	Jan 1 1835- Jul 31 1850	MFGS 51/008-09
General Register	Jul 31 1850- Dec 31 1860	MFGS 51/009- 010
General Register	Jan 1 1861- Dec 1878	MFGS 51/001, 148, 010
General Register (Males Only)	Dec 9 1878- Sep 25 1884	MFGS 51/014-15
General Register(Males Only)	Sep 27 1884- Aug 20 1887	MFGS 51/015-16
General Register (Males Only)	Sep 8 1890- Dec 31 1896	MFGS 51/016-17
General Register (Males Only)	Jan 1 1897- Dec 30 1899	MFGS 51/017-18

Cork County Jail continued

Record Type	Dates Covered	Reference No.
Description Register (males and females)	Nov 23 1870- Dec 9 1878	MFGS 51/ 023-024
General Register(Females Only)	Jan 1 1879- May 11 1880	MFGS 51/ 020
General Register(Females Only)	Jan 2 1882- Dec 31 1890	MFGS 51/ 020-21
General Register(Females Only)	Jan 1 1891- Dec 31 1901	MFGS 51/ 021-22
Register of males and females committed from petty sessions	Oct 7 1847- 1849	MFGS 51/ 024-25
Register of males and females committed from petty sessions	Oct 19 1850- Sep 15 1851	MFGS 51/ 025
Register of Debtors	Jan 9 1858- Dec 28 1872	MFGS 51/ 025
Register of male juveniles, aged 16 and over	Jan 1 1979- Jul 19 1915	MFGS 51/ 023
Register of Prisoners with Previous convictions	Nov 8 1878- Apr 15 1901	MFGS 51/ 024

Cork County Jail continued

Record Type	Dates Covered	Reference No.
Register of Convicted Prisoners	Aug 23 1823- Dec 31 1844	MFGS 51/010-11
House of Correction Journal	May 27 1824- Dec 31 1837	MFGS 51/023
Register of Prisoners Committed from Petty Sessions	Oct 7 1847- Oct 17 1849	MFGS 51/024-25
Ledger on Court Decisions (petty to serious)	Jun 16 1830- May 21 1834	MFGS 51/013
Ledger on Court Decisions	May 27 1834- Apr 9 1839	MFGS 51/014
Ledger on Court Decisions	Mar 20 1847- Jun 7 1848	MFGS 51/014
Ledger on Court Decisions	Mar 24 1850- Mar 7 1852	MFGS 51/014
General Register	Jan 1 1835- Jul 31 1850	MFGS 51/008-09
General Register	Jul 31 1850- Dec 31 1860	MFGS 51/009- 010
General Register	Jan 1 1861- Dec 1878	MFGS 51/001, 148, 010
General Register (Males Only)	Dec 9 1878- Sep 25 1884	MFGS 51/014-15
General Register(Males Only)	Sep 27 1884- Aug 20 1887	MFGS 51/015-16

Record Type	Dates Covered	Reference No.
General Register (Males Only)	Sep 8 1890- Dec 31 1896	MFGS 51/016-17
General Register (Males Only)	Jan 1 1897- Dec 30 1899	MFGS 51/017-18

Ennis Inebriates Reformatory

Record Type	Dates Covered	Reference No.
General register	Apr 24 1900- Mar 3 1916	MFGS 51/079
Register of treatment, before and after	1902-1920	
Index of inmates	1899-1918	

Fort Carlisle Convict Depot, Cork Harbour

Record Type	Dates Covered	Reference No.
Convict Depot (males)	Oct 4 1848-Nov 20 1867	MFGS 51/079-80

Galway Jail

Record Type	Dates Covered	Reference No.
General Register	Jan 1 1839- Aug 31 1851	MFGS 51/155
General Register	Sep 9 1848- Mar 15 1858	MFGS 51/080
General Register	Sep 1 1851- Dec 30 1864	MFGS 51/156
General Register	Mar 18 1858- Dec 31 1875	MFGS 51/156-7
Register of Untried Prisoners	Nov 20 1848- Oct 20 1876	MFGS 51/080-81
General Register	Jun 12 1865- Dec 31 1875	MFGS 51/157
General Register	Jan 1 1876- Oct 1878	MFGS 51/157-158
General Register	Oct 6 1878- Oct 11 1880	MFGS 51/081
General Register	Oct 12 1880- Dec 30 1885	MFGS 51/081-2
General Register	Jan 1886- 1892	MFGS 51/081
General Register	Apr 20 1892- Nov 11 1899	MFGS 51/082
General Register	Nov 11 1899- Sep 24 1906	MFGS 51/082-3
Register of Male Juveniles	Jan 7 1864- Jan 16 1879	MFGS 51/081

Grangegorman Women's Prison

Record Type	Dates Covered	Reference No.
Register of Vagrants	Feb 25 1850- Jun 2 1851	MFGS 51/039
Register of Vagrants	Dec 17 1853- Jun 2 1855	MFGS 51/039
Register of Drunkards	Jan 3 1839- Jul 13 1840	MFGS 51/037
Register of Drunkards	Dec 18 1848- Nov 16 1855	MFGS 51/037-8
Register of Drunkards	Jan 9 1861- Dec 31 1869	MFGS 51/038
Register of Drunkards	Oct 22 1875- Jul 22 1880	MFGS 51/038-9
Register of Juveniles	Jul 1 1853-Dec 31 1855	MFGS 51/041
Register of Juveniles (mal/ fem)	Jul 2 1855- Nov 28 1877	MFGS 51/040
Register of Petty Male Prisoners	Aug 1 1881- May 17 1883	MFGS 51/041
General Register	Dec 19 1831- Sep 1838	MFGS 51/027
General Register	Sep 14 1838- Dec 31 1840	MFGS 51/027 -8
General Register	Jan 1 1841- Dec 31 1841	MFGS 51/148
General Register	Jan 1 1844- 31 Dec 1845	MFGS 51/028

Record Type	Dates Covered	Reference No.
General Register	Jan 5 1849- Dec 31 1849	MFGS 51/028
General Register	Jan 1 1850- Dec 31 1851	MFGS 51/028-29
General Register	Jan 1 1853- Dec 31 1853	MFGS 51/029
General Register	Jan 1 1855- Dec 31 1856	MFGS 51/029
General Register	Jan 2 1864- Jan 10 1865	MFGS 51/030
General Register	Jul 24 1879- Mar 14 1885	MFGS 51/031-32
Register of Prisoners Committed for Trial	Jan 2 1854- Jan 14 1865	MFGS 51/150-151
Prisoners Committed for Further Examination	Oct 30 1877- Oct 31 1883	MFGS 51/040
Register of Prisoners Known to be Discharged Convicts	Jan 5 1871- Aug 4 1896	MFGS 51/140
Court Trial Book (Register of prisoners for Trial)	Mar 6 1850- Dec 22 1851	MFGS 51/039-40
Court Trial Book	Jan 13 1852- Dec 23 1852	MFGS 51/040
Court Trial Book	Jan 8 1855- Dec 6 1858	MFGS 51/040

Court Trial Book	Dec 20 1867- Aug 12 1874	MFGS 51/040
Court Trial Book	Aug 28 1871- Dec 1 1883	MFGS 51/149
Court Trial Book	Oct 2 1874- Nov 15 1882	MFGS 51/040

Kilkenny Jail

Record Type	Dates Covered	Reference No.
General Register	1892-1898	MFGS 51/143

Kilmainham Jail

Record Type	Dates	Reference No.
Treason felony and General register	1798-1814	MFGS 51/042
General register	Feb 16 1815-Dec 30 1823	MFGS 51/052
General register	1830-1834	MFGS 51/042
General register	1835-1837. Jan 1838-June 20 1840. June 21 1840-Jan 16 1843. Jan 2 1843- Dec 31 1845. Jan 2 1846-Jun 12 1848 (named index) June 1848- Mar 30 1850 .	MFGS 51/043

Record Type	Dates	Reference No.
Register of Convicts (males)	Nov 28 1836-Nov 3 1840. Jul 2 1840-Jun 24 1850	MFGS 51/050
General register	Oct 23 1850-Nov 18 1853.	MFGS 51/147
General register	Mar 1850-Oct 22 1850 Nov 18 1850- Sep 1 1858 Sep 4 1858-Dec 31 1863 Jan 2 1864- Aug 27 1867 Aug 28 1867- Oct 26 1871	MFGS 51/044
General register	Oct 26 1871-Sep 20 1875 Sep 20 1875-Apr 1 1878 Apr 1 1878- Oct 10 1881 Oct 13 1881-Jul 31 1883	MFGS 51/045
General register	Aug 1 1883- Aug 31 1888 Aug 1 1893-Oct 13 1894	MFGS 51/046
Debtor's register	August 11 1845 - September 27 1881	MFGS 51/050
General register	Aug 1 1883- Aug 31 1888 Sep 1 1888- Jul 31 1893 Aug 1 1893-Oct 13 1894	MFGS 51/046
General register	Oct 13 1894- Sep 29 1898 Oct 1 1898- Dec 31 1903	MFGS 51/047
General register	Jan 1 1904-Sep 30 1908 Oct 1 1908- Feb 28 1910	MFGS 51/048
Remand prisoners	Jul 1 1892-May 30 1894 Jun 1 1894- Jan 6 1896 Jan 1 1896-98	MFGS 51/048 MFGS 51/048-9

Record Type	Dates	Reference No.
Remand prisoners	Nov 9 1900-Nov 6 1905 Nov 1 1905- May 31 1909	MFGS 51/049 MFGS 51/049-50
Remand prisoners	Jan 1 1909- Feb 28 1910	MFGS 51/050
Prisoners awaiting trial at Green Street Court	1883-1892	MFGS 51/051
Prisoners with previous convictions	1883-1885 1898-1899	MFGS 51/050-1 MFGS 51/051
Male juveniles	Jul 2 1855-8 Jul 1878	MFGS 51/050

Limerick Jail

Record Type	Dates Covered	Reference No.
General Register	Apr 1838- Dec 1847	MFGS 51/085
Register of debtors	Sep 19 1835- Feb 28 1881	MFGS 51/085
General Register of criminals sentenced in Spring Assizes	1830- 1837	MFGS 51/084-85
General Register of criminals sentenced in Spring Assizes	1837- 1858	MFGS 51/085

Record Type	Dates Covered	Reference No.
General Register	Jan 1 1855- Dec 31 1867	MFGS 51/086
General Register	Jan 1 1867- Dec 31 1874	MFGS 51/086
General Register	Mar 13 1874- Aug 8 1878	MFGS 51/087
General Register	Jun 26 1877- Dec 31 1880	MFGS 51/087
General Register (Females)	Sep 1878- Jan 8 1896	MFGS 51/087,88,89
General Register(Males)	Jan 1 1881- Nov 1 1885	MFGS 51/087-88
General Register(Males)	Nov 2 1885- Dec 31 1888	MFGS 51/088-89
General Register(Males)	Jan 1 1889- 1894	MFGS 51/089-90
General Register of Prisoners	Jan 5 1899- Dec 31 1901	MFGS 51/90-91
Register of summary convictions	Nov 16 1861- Dec 31 1868	MFGS 51/086

Longford Jail

Record Type	Dates Covered	Reference No.
General Register	Jul 9 1856- Dec 23 1868	MFGS 51/158

Mountjoy Jail

Record Type	Dates Covered	Reference No.
Register of Male Convicts	Jul 24 1845- Jul 14 1847	MFGS 51/052
Register of Male Convicts	Mar 27 1850- Aug 13 1855	MFGS 51/053
Register of Convicts for Transportation	1848- 1850	MFGS 51/065
General Register of Female convicts, (Cork Gaol until Aug 1858)	Oct 20 1854- Oct 28 1886	MFGS 51/057
Male convicts	Jan 3 1860- Apr 1866	MFGS 51/053, 151
Male Convicts	Jul 29 1867- Mar 11 1875	MFGS 51/152
Male Convicts	Jun 29 1875- Nov 22 1880	MFGS 51/152-153
Male Convicts	Sep 6 1880- Aug 10 1888	MFGS 51/153, 058
Convict Classification Register	1855- 1880	MFGS 51/059-60
Convict Classification Register	1857- 1861	MFGS 51/061
Convict Classification Register	1857- 1866	MFGS 51/062

Record Type	Dates Covered	Reference No.
Convict Classification Register	1875- 1884	MFGS 51/063,64,65
Convict Classification Register (females)	1868- 1875	MFGS 51/065-66
Convict Classification Register (Females)	1875- 1882	MFGS 51/066

Naas Jail

Record Type	Dates	Reference No.
General Register	Jan 1 1859- Dec 31 1864	MFGS 51/ 160-161
General Register	Jan 1 1865 Jun 21 1867	MFGS 51/ 161- 162
General Register	Jun 28 1867 Oct 25 1871 (8 pages missing)	MFGS 51/ 162
General Register	Apr 29 1875- Nov 21 1881	MFGS 51/ 092

Nenagh Jail

Record Type	Dates	Reference No.
General register	Jul 26 1842- Jun 11 1847	MFGS 51/092
General register	Mar 31 1848- Apr 26 1852	MFGS 51/092-3
General register	Jan 2 1863- Dec 10 1874	MFGS 51/162-3
General register	Dec 10 1874- June 28 1877	MFGS 51/093
General register	Nov 15 1878- Mar 27 1884	
Register of Debtors	1843- 1872	MFGS 51/092

Newgate Jail

Record Type	Dates	Reference No.
General register	Jan 1845-Dec 31 1847	MFGS 51/068
General register	Jan 26 1848-Dec 31 1850	MFGS 51/068-9
General register	Mar 1 1849-Jun 24 1858	MFGS 51/067
Convict Classification register	1855-56 (males) 1857-58 (females)	MFGS 51/069
Convict Classification register	1856-61(males)	MFGS 51/069-70

Philipstown Convict Depot

Record Type	Dates Covered	Reference No.
General Register	1849 - 1862	GPO PN 3
Character Books	1847- 1862	GPO PN 4 &5

Richmond Bridewell, Dublin

Record Type	Dates	Reference No.
Register of female prisoners	1830- Dec 3 1836	MFGS 51/140
General register(males)	Sep 1845-Sep 30 1847	MFGS 51/067
Convict Depot (males)	May 5 1847-May 24 1883	MFGS 51/077
General register(males)	Jan 1 1851- Dec 31 1851	MFGS 51/067
Prisoners committed for trial	Jan 1 1851- Dec 31 1855	MFGS 51/070
general register(males)	Jan 1 1852- Dec 30 1852	MFGS 51/067
general register(males)	Jan 1 1853- Oct 25 1853	MFGS 51/071
Prisoners for trial who had been in	Jan 13 1852- Jan 13 1853	MFGS 51/071
Court register of prisoners for trial	Jul 11 1854- Jun 13 1855?	MFGS 51/071
Court register of prisoners for trial	Aug 14 1855- Jan 9 1863	MFGS 51/071
General register	Jan 1 1856- Oct 23 1858	MFGS 51/072
General register	Jan 1 1856- May 20 1865	MFGS 51/070 MFGS 51/072
General register	Jan 1 1859-Nov 15 1860	MFGS 51/070 MFGS 51/072

Record Type	Dates	Reference No.
Register of military prisoners	Jan 5 1855- Nov 11 1863	
Register of convicted prisoners	Jun 15 1861- Mar 1863	MFGS 51/072
Register of convicted prisoners	Aug 22 1861- Apr 2 1866	MFGS 51/073
Register of convicted prisoners	Mar 11 1863- Aug 22 1864	MFGS 51/072
Register of drunkards	Jan 1 1861- Sep 1873	MFGS 51/073
Court register of prisoners for trial at quarter sessions	Jun 14 1861- Apr 3 1867	MFGS 51/072
Register of previously convicted prisoners for trial	Jun 9 1863- Jun 18 1867	MFGS 51073
Register of convicts	Jun 27 1864- Feb 27 1883	MFGS 51/078
Prisoners committed for trial	May 30 1865- Dec 6 1873	MFGS 51/154
Register of convicted prisoners	May 25 1866- Dec 31 1867	MFGS 51/073
Register of convicted prisoners	Jan 1867- Jun 1869	
Court register of prisoners for trial at quarter sessions	Oct 8 1867- Apr 1871?	MFGS 51/154
Register of convicted prisoners	Jun 30 1869- Dec 29 1870	MFGS 51/073
Register of convicted prisoners	Jan 2 1871- Aug 19 1872	MFGS 51/074
Register of previously convicted prisoners for trial	Mar 7 1871- Jul 17 1874	MFGS 51/074

Record Type	Dates	Reference No.
Register of previously convicted prisoners for trial	May 1872. Feb 4 1877?- 8	MFGS 51/075
Register of prisoners for trial	May 14 1872 - Oct 13 1876	MFGS 51/074
Register of convicted prisoners	Aug 20 1872- Nov 3 1873	MFGS 51/074
Register of convicted prisoners	Nov 3 1873- Mar 4 1875	MFGS 51/074
Register of convicted prisoners	Mar 13 1875- Mar 4 1878	MFGS 51/075
Register of convicted prisoners	Mar 5 1878-Sep 1880	MFGS 51/075
General register	Sep 20 1880- Sep 27 1882	MFGS 51/075
general register	Sep 27 1882- Dec 31 1884	MFGS 51/076
General register	Jan 1 1885- Jul 10 1886	MFGS 51/076
General register	Jul 12 1886- May 13 1887	MFGS 51/077
General register	May 13 1887- Apr 4 1888 (Mountjoy from Apr 2 1888)	MFGS 51/077

Smithfield Convict Depot

Record Type	Dates Covered	Reference No.
General Register (Males)	Apr 1 1844- Aug 24 1849	MFGS 51/078

Tralee Jail

Record Type	Dates Covered	Reference No.
General Register	Jun 25 1852- Dec 31 1866	MFGS 51/ 099
General Register	Nov 1 1888- Apr 23 1894	MFGS 51/ 099-100
General Register	Apr 23 1894- Dec 28 1900	MFGS 51/ 100

Trim Jail

Record Type	Dates Covered	Reference No.
Committals for Quarter Sessions	Aug 1837- Apr 1844	MFGS 51/103
Trim Sessions Calendar	July 1 1842	MFGS 51/103
Duleek Quarter Sessions	June 17 1842	MFGS 51/103
General Register	1837- 1849	MFGS 51/103
General Register	1852-1878	MFGS 51/104

Wexford Jail

Record Type	Dates Covered	Reference No.
Register of Criminals	Jan 2 1852- Dec 7 1874	MFGS 51/114,121
Register of Criminals	Jan 4 1875- Sep 21 1878	MFGS 51/121
General Register	Sep 23 1878- Mar 30 1885	MFGS 51/119
General Register	Apr 2 1885- Dec 30 1899	MFGS 51/119-120
General Register	Jan 2 1900- Sep 28 1904	MFGS 51/120

Wicklow Jail

Record Type	Dates Covered	Reference No.
Register of Criminal Offenders	May 29 1846- Mar 12 1851	MFGS 51/ 121-122
Register of Previous Offenders	Dec 22 1849- Dec 3 1856	MFGS 51/ 120
Register of Convicts	Jul 11 1848- Jan 4 1880	MFGS 51/ 121
Register of Criminal Offenders	Jun 7 1861- Dec 31 1878	MFGS 51/ 122-123

Record Type	Dates Covered	Reference No.
Register of Offenders jailed in default of Fine Payment	Jul 16 1864- Jul 10 1893	MFGS 51/ 120
General Register	Jan 2 1879- Dec 1880	MFGS 51/ 120
General Register	Aug 2 1890- Dec 26 1901	MFGS 51/ 124

Appendix 2. Available Jail Registers with Named Indexes

Athy,Kildare

Record Indexed	Dates Covered	Reference No.
General Register	Aug 5 1848- Dec 30 1855	MFGS 51/052-53
General Register	Jan 2 1858 - Feb 14 1860 (Letter E missing)	MFGS 51/001

Carrick

Register Type	Dates Covered	Reference No.
General Register	1845-1855	MFGS 51/002
General Register	1863-1868 (Letter M only)	MFGS 51/002
General Register	1869-1878	MFGS 51/002

Cork County Jail

Record Indexed	Dates Covered	Reference No.
General Register	1826-1840	MFGS 51/012
General Register	1843- 1854	MFGS 51/013
General Register	1862-1886	MFGS 51/013

Ennis Inebriate Reformatory

Record Indexed	Dates Covered	Reference No.
General Register	1899-1918	MFGS 51/079

Galway Jail

Record Indexed	Dates Covered	Reference No.
Female Prisoners	1896-1900	MFGS 51/084
General Register	1899-1905	MFGS 51/084

Grangegorman,Dublin

Record Indexed	Dates Covered	Reference No.
Drunkards	1878-1880	MFGS 51/041
General Register	1880-1882	MFGS 51/042
General Register	1883 (A-F missing)	MFGS 51/041
General Register	1887	MFGS 51/041

Record Indexed	Dates Covered	Reference No.
General Register	1889	MFGS 51/041-042
General Register	1891	MFGS 51/042
General Register	1893-1895	MFGS 51/042
General Register	1897-1898	MFGS 51/042

Kilmainham, Dublin

Record Indexed	Dates Covered	Reference
General register	1845	MFGS 51/043
Male prisoners	1879	MFGS 51/040
General register	1873-1876 1881-1883 1885-1887 1888-1891 1893-1895	MFGS 51/051 MFGS 51/051-2 MFGS 51/051
General register	1892-1895	MFGS 51/052
Untried prisoners	1892-1895 1896-1900 1904-1908 1909-1910	MFGS 51/052
Male prisoners	1901-1905	MFGS 51/140

Limerick Jail

Record Indexed	Dates Covered	Reference No.
Male Prisoners	1887-1899	MFGS 51/091
Female Prisoners	1890-1895	MFGS 51/091

Mountjoy,Dublin

Record Indexed	Dates Covered	Reference No.
General Register(Males)	1896-1898 1899-1903	MFGS 51/139
General Register(Females)	1892 1894	MFGS 51/139-140 MFGS 51/140
Females on Remand	1897-1906	MFGS 51/139

Richmond Bridewell ,Dublin

Record Indexed	Dates Covered	Reference No.
Female Felons	1831-Dec 1836	MFGS 51/140
General Register (B-F only)	1845-1855	MFGS 51/067
Prisoners for Further Examination	1855-1863	MFGS 51/078
General Register	1866-1867	MFGS 51/078
General Register	1878-1881	MFGS 51/078 *

Record Indexed	Dates Covered	Reference No.
General Register	1886	MFGS 51/078-079 *
Habitual Criminal Register	1881-1883	MFGS 51/078

* Possibly Mountjoy.

Sligo

Record Indexed	Dates Covered	Reference No.
General register	1857-68	MFGS 51/095

Tralee

Record Indexed	Dates Covered	Reference No.
General Register	1879-1886	MFGS 51/102
Female Prisoners	1891-1920	MFGS 51/102
Male Prisoners	1887-1891	MFGS 51/102
Male Prisoners	1898-1904	MFGS 51/102

Tullamore

Record Indexed	Dates Covered	Reference No.
General Register	1888-1907	MFGS 51/106

Waterford

Record Indexed	Dates Covered	Reference No.
General Register	1893-1899	MFGS 51/119

Wexford

Record Indexed	Dates Covered	Reference No.
General Register	1879-1887	MFGS 51/120
General Register	1892-1902	MFGS 51/120

Appendix 3 : List of surviving Bridewell records and Dates Covered

Bridewells	
Bandon	1856-1878
Charleville	1856-1880
Clonakilty	1883-1886
Dunmanway	1855-1878
Fermoy	1897-1909
Kanturk	1855-1878
Kinsale	1856-1879
Loughrea	1884-1920
Millstreet	1855-1862
Mitchelstown	1884-1892
New Ross	1846-1905
Queenstown	1882-1894
Skibbereen	1855-1881
Youghal	1873-1900

Appendix 4

(a)Types of Prisons:

1.County and City Jails
2.Bridewells
3.Government/Convict Prisons (Mountjoy, Maryborough, Spike Island)
4.Convict Depots (Fort Carlisle, Newgate, Grangegorman, Philipstown, Kilmainham)
5. Intermediate Prisons (Lusk)

(b)Jails examined for this project:

1 Athy
2 Naas
3 Carrick (partially)
4 Castlebar
5 Clonmel
6 Tralee
7 Trim
8 Richmond Bridewell
9 Grangegorman Women's Prison
10 Mountjoy (partially)
11 Newgate
12 Phillipstown
13 Sligo
14 Fort Carlisle
15 Smithfield Convict Depot
16 Kilmainham
17 Skibereen Bridewell
18 Fermoy Bridewell
19 Maryborough
20 Queen's County Jail
21 Ennis Inebriate Reformatory

22 Limerick (partially)
23 Galway(partially)
24 Longford (partially)

(c)Types of Prison Records Found

General Registers - most common.
Debtor Registers - Kilmainham, Sligo, Nenagh, Limerick, Cork.
Drunkard Registers - Grangegorman, Richmond Bridewell.
Register of Vagrants - poor survival rate. Grangegorman only.
Customs and Excise Offenders - Poor survival rate. Sligo
Military Offenders- Richmond Bridewell. Also garrison towns like Clonmel, Athy, Naas worth investigating.
Juvenile Registers - Clonmel . Grangegorman.
Alcoholic Registers (Ennis Inebriate Reformatory)
Habitual Offenders Registers - from 1869. More detailed than General Register.
Lunatic Registers - Richmond Lunatic Asylum via Grangegorman. Often records prisoner state of mind and means of support.
Convict Registers - Mountjoy, Grangegorman, Philipstown, Fort Carlisle.
Convict Classification Registers - detailed particulars on behaviour while in custody. Mountjoy. Philipstown.

Appendix 5

Register of Debtors Kilmainham Gaol Dublin
From 11 Aug 1845 - 2 Aug 1867. [147]

Debtor name	Date committed	Amount	Plaintiff	Discharged By	Process of Committal
Thomas Lewen	26 April 1845	£47.11.6	John Darcy	Insolvent Court	Queen's Bench
Henry Gould	3rd Mar 1846	£48.13.2	Edwd Sullivan	High Sheriff	Exchequer Execution
same		£73.18.3	John A Surfles	High Sheriff	Exchequer Execution
same		£44.9.6	James Gallagher	High Sheriff	Exchequer Execution
Andrew Blake	6th June 1846	£27.2.2	Michael Keane	Insolvent Court	Exchequer Execution
Charles Parry	14th Jan 1847	£41.10.10	Geo Henry Houghton	Insolvent Court	Exchequer Execution
James Lewis Flanigan	4th Mar 1847	£9.0.4	John Darcy	Insolvent Court	Co. Dublin Decree
Henry Cunningham Kelly	16th Mar 1847	£5.15.3	? Lewis Savage	Insolvent Court	Co. Dublin Decree
same		£20.9.11	Charles Marsh	Insolvent Court	Co. Dublin Decree

---

[147] National Archives of Ireland , Bishop Street Dublin. MFGS 51/050.

Debtor name	Date committed	Amount	Plaintiff	Discharged By	Process of Committal
Percy ? Penrose Jessop	31st Mar 1847	£111.1.1	Robert Montgomery	Insolvent Court	City of Dublin Decree
Charles Brabazon	6th April 1847	£19.10.5	Michael ? Lawlor	Insolvent Court	Queen's Bench Decree
John Cluskey	1st May 1847	£15.17.4	William Minchin	Insolvent Court	Co. Dublin Decree
James McGrane	17 May 1847	£181.18.14	John Price Eaton	Insolvent Court	Queen's Bench Exec'n
Thomas Reilly	25 May 1847	£11.5.4	Par Pur ?Molloy	Insolvent Court	Co. Dublin Decree
same	same	£11.5.4	same	Insolvent Court	Co. Dublin Decree
same	same	£10.19.10	Peter Finegan	Insolvent Court	Co. Dublin Decree
same	same	£12.19.11	Par Pur ?Molloy	Insolvent Court	Co. Dublin Decree
same	same	£12.19.11	same	Insolvent Court	Co. Dublin Decree
same	same	£12.19.11	same	Insolvent Court	Co. Dublin Decree

Debtor name	Date committed	Amount	Plaintiff	Discharged By	Process of Committal
Henry Moore Cairnes	9 June 1847	£36.7.3	Wm Atkinson	Insolvent Court	Queen's Bench
same	11 June 1847	£3.2.11	J. Moore	Insolvent Court	City of Dublin Decree
West Archer	25 June 1847	£26.7.5	Alex Terrance Holland	Dead	Exchequer Execution
Thomas Gallagher	9 July 1847	£6.8.8	Patrick R Keogh	Died	Co. Dublin Decree
Mortimer Mills Byrne	12 July 1847	£2.9.11	Rev. Thos Kingston	Insolvent Court	Co. Dublin Decree
same	19 July 1847	£10.17.10	Figgis Oldham	Insolvent Court	Co. Dublin Decree
same	30 July 1847	£6.9.4	Peter Coperly	Insolvent Court	Co. Dublin Decree
Rev. Charles McDonald	19 July 1847	£20.11.4	John Darcy	Insolvent Court	Co. Dublin Decree
same	same	£9.11.4	Phelan & Mahon?	Insolvent Court	Co. Dublin Decree
William Moore	29 July 1847	£4.18.4	J B Mulhall	Plaintiff	City of Dublin Decree

Debtor name	Date committed	Amount	Plaintiff	Discharged By	Process of Committal
Joseph Walker	10 Aug 1847	£6.0.1	Pat Duffy	Plaintiff	Seneschal Decree
Bernard McDonagh	11 Aug 1847	£20.19.4	Patrick Byrne	Insolvent Court	Exchequer Execution
Saunders Carroll	20 July 1847	£73.18.1	J Jervis & F Barry	Insolvent Court	Exchequer Execution
James S Talbot	22 Sep 1847	£7.10.2	J Madden	Insolvent Court	City of Dublin Decree
Alfred Walker	11 Oct 1847	£3.14.3	Henry Bayley	Insolvent Court	Seneschal Decree
George Kendrick	19 Nov 1847	£12.9.4	Philip Lynch	Insolvent Court	Co. Dublin Decree
Richard Williams	22 Nov 1847	£91.9.10	Henry Eugene Perrin Wright	Insolvent Court	Queen's Bench Exec'n
same	same	£58.19.7	Thomas Johnston	Insolvent Court	Exchequer Execution
Alexander Kyle	12 May 1846	£9000	The Queen	Plaintiff	Exchequer Execution
Michael O'Meara Brennan	28 May 1846	£39.13.9	Henry McDona	Habeus Corpus	Queen's Bench Exec'n

Irish Nineteenth Century Prison Records: survey and evaluation

Debtor name	Date committed	Amount	Plaintiff	Discharged By	Process of Committal
same	21 Oct 1847	£366.6.7	John Connor	Four Courts	Common Pleas Exec'n
John Langley	10 Jun 1847	£59.0.5	Henry E Stephen	Sub Sheriff	Queen's Bench Exec'n
Hugh Carroll	27 Aug 1847	£8.16.8	Michael Byrne	Insolvent Court	Co. Wicklow Decree
Walter Henry Mansfield	21 Sep 1847	£40.7.3	Daniel Beare?	Sub Sheriff	Exchequer Execution
Richard Corbally	22 Sep 1847	£20.8.4	Pat Fitzpatrick	Died	Co. Dublin Decree
Patrick McEntagart	27 Oct 1847	£1.13.4	Michael Fagan	Died	Co. Dublin Decree
Bridget O'Kelly	30 Oct 1847	£13.11.2	Thomas Ashby	Sheriff under nisi pris chap. 28	Exchequer Execution
Anne Revell	11 Nov 1847	£1.9.3	John W'm White	Insolvent Court	St. Mary's Abbey Decree
Robert Sandys	11 Nov 1847	£4.8.4	Jane Glynn	Plaintiff Attorney	Co. Dublin Decree

120

Debtor name	Date committed	Amount	Plaintiff	Discharged By	Process of Committal
Lorenzo Triggea	25 Nov 1847	£5.0.0	Jane Glynn	Sessions Court	Forfeited Recognizance
George Kershaw	10 Dec 1847	£3.16.3	Alex Findlater	Plaintiff Attorney	Co. Dublin Decree
Flemming Pinkston O'Reilly	21 Dec 1847	£211.16.7	Executrixes of W'm Tucker	Habeus Corpus	Exchequer Execution
James Cullen	22 Dec 1847	£13.9.4	John Thos? Cook	Habeus Corpus	City of Dublin Decree
Catherine Lamb	27 Dec 1847	£1.18.10	Thomas Johnson	Plaintiff Attorney	Co. Dublin Decree
Barry Farrell	27 Dec 1847	£2.7.1	Bernard Tier	Plaintiff Attorney	Co. Dublin Decree
Patrick Donnelly	28 Dec 1847	£1.13.4	Catherine Smith	Plaintiff	Co. Dublin Decree
John Thomas La Bel	4 Jan 1848	£6.18.4	Thomas Boylan	Insolvent Court	Co. Dublin Decree
same	11 jan 1848	£4.16.10	Richard and Joseph Matthews	Insolvent Court	Co. Dublin Decree

Debtor name	Date committed	Amount	Plaintiff	Discharged By	Process of Committal
William Palmer	13 Jan 1848	£10.0.0		Sessions Court	Green Wax forfeited recognizance
Thomas Palmer	13 Jan 1848	£17.1.2	Thomas Johnson	Insolvent Court	Co. Dublin Decree
Thomas Graham	18 Jan 1848	£8.11.11	John McVeagh	Plaintiff Attorney	Co. Tyrone Decree
James Murphy	19 Jan 1848	£12.1.9	Edwd Stephens	Insolvent Court	City of Dublin Decree
John Manning	19 Jan 1848	£8.7.4	Patrick McCabe	Insolvent Court	Co. Dublin Decree
Henry Maxwell Bristow	21 Jan 1848	£302.8.10	The Queen	Collector of Excise	Co. Dublin Decree
James Hanlon	25 Jan 1848	£2.7.10	John Doran	Plaintiff Attorney	Co. Dublin Decree
Patrick Hanlon	25 Jan 1848	£1.16.4	John Doran	Plaintiff Attorney	Co. Dublin Decree
John Clancy	31 Jan 1848	£2.9.6	Thomas Arkins	Insolvent Court	St. Mary's Abbey Decree
Ellen Walker	1 Feb 1848	£8.18.8	Archibald Frew	Plaintiff	St. Mary's Abbey Decree

Debtor name	Date committed	Amount	Plaintiff	Discharged By	Process of Committal
John Clancy	2 Feb 1848	£5.3.0	O'Neill Stewart	Insolvent Court	St. Mary's Abbey Decree
Charles Everard	5 Feb 1848	£6.2.4	Johnston & Sharpley	Plaintiff Attorney	Co. Dublin Decree
Mathew Finglas	7 Feb 1848	£1.17.4	William Boileau	Insolvent Court	City of Dublin Decree
James Gerity	8 Feb 1848	£49.11.3	Isaac Hill	Insolvent Court	Queen's Bench Exec'n
Miles Byrnes	15 Feb 1848	£14.18.4	Mathew McGrath	Insolvent Court	Co. Dublin Decree
Lawrence Dowling	15 Feb 1848	£1.4.11	Anthony Power	Plaintiff	Co. Kildare Decree
Eleanor Knox	19 Feb 1848	£230.15.10	John Robinson	Insolvent Court	Queen's Bench Decree
Mary Ann Sheil	24 Feb 1848	£129.15.0	Archer Coats	Sub Sheriff	Queen's Bench Decree
William Walker	3 Mar 1848	£8.14.10	John Clarke	Plaintiff Attorney	Co. Dublin Decree

Debtor name	Date committed	Amount	Plaintiff	Discharged By	Process of Committal
Elizabeth Murray	7 Mar 1848	£2.19.11	Eleanor Burke	Plaintiff ?	St. Mary's Abbey Decree
Thomas Quinn	10 Mar 1848	£1.4.4	John Lavaria	Plaintiff	Co. Dublin Decree
Robert Shea Booth	10 Mar 1848	£14.1.0	Edwd Dowling	Plaintiff Attorney	Co. Dublin Decree
Same Robert Sherlock	10 Mar 1848	£17.9.4	Moses Whitty	Plaintiff Attorney	Co. Dublin Decree
William Figgis	10 Mar 1848	£31.19.10	James & John Cummins	Sheriff	Exchequer Execution
James Fitzgerald	13 Mar 1848	£3.9.4	Eliz & Christian Williamson	Plaintiff Attorney	Co. Dublin Decree
Rev. John D. Hirst	13 Mar 1848	£4.13.10	James Wright	Plaintiff Attorney	Co. Dublin Decree
Francis Henry Fitzgerald	15 Mar 1848	£45.1.8	Joseph Fletcher the younger	Insolvent Court	Judges Fiat
Alfred F Armstrong	23 Mar 1848	£4.17.4	James Moran	Plaintiff Attorney	City of Dublin Decree

Debtor name	Date committed	Amount	Plaintiff	Discharged By	Process of Committal
Alexander Rosborough	28 Mar 1848	£7.15.2	Mary Emily Daly	Insolvent Court	Co. Dublin Decree
John Gaffney	29 Mar 1848	£20.7.4	Mark Doran	Insolvent Court	Co. Dublin Decree
Michael Cullen	1 Apr 1848	£7.5.4	John Ferguson	Plaintiff	City of Dublin Decree
James C Powell	3 Apr 1848	£8.7.0	Francis Hamilton	Insolvent Court	Co. Dublin Decree
Thomas McEvoy	6 Apr 1848	£5.14.0	John Ferguson	Plaintiff Attorney	City of Dublin Decree
Eliz. Jane Doyne	7 Apr 1848	£53.3.4	William Egan	Sheriff	Queen's Bench Exec'n
Same	7 Apr 1848	£50.17.11	Peter W. Murphy	Henry Davis Executors	Exchequer Execution
Luke Mordant	8 Apr 1848	£2.11.4	Peter Casserly	Insolvent Court	Co. Dublin Decree
Michael Church	10 Mar 1848	£3.11.10	Patrick Fitzpatrick	Plaintiff Attorney	Co. Dublin Decree
Thomas Harford	13 Mar 1848	£2.16.4	Patrick Curtin	Plaintiff Attorney	Co. Dublin Decree

Debtor name	Date committed	Amount	Plaintiff	Discharged By	Process of Committal
William Edmund Burke	13 Mar 1848	£7.8.11	Sarah McDermot	Insolvent Court	Seneschal Decree, Mary's Abbey
Sarah Behan	17 Mar 1848	£13.17.0	John Yeates	Insolvent Court	Grange-gor- man Decree
Richard Frederick Waters	21 Mar 1848	£34.4.10	Stephen Alcock	Insolvent Court	Exchequer Execution
Eleanor Donnellan	22 Mar 1848	£3.19.4	William Collins	Plaintiff Attorney	Co. Dublin Decree
Bridget Connolly	27 Mar 1848	£2.2.9	Charles O'Brien	Plaintiff	St. Mary's Abbey De-cree
Patrick Callaghan	27 Mar 1848	£8.2.3	Bernard Tier	Insolvent Court	Co. Dublin Decree
Dominic Rooney	27 Mar 1848	£7.14.7	Timothy O'Brien	Insolvent Court	Co. Dublin Decree
Same	27 Mar 1848	£13.9.5	Alicia Forde	Insolvent Court	Co. Dublin Decree
Michael Foley	28 Mar 1848	£1.14.10	James Wright		Co. Dublin Decree
John Keatinge	1 May 1848	£4.8.4	John Gal-lie & John Oulton	Sheriff	Co. Dublin Decree

Debtor name	Date committed	Amount	Plaintiff	Discharged By	Process of Committal
Priscilla McLoughlin	4 May 1848	£5.2.0	Thomas Hickey	Insolvent Court	Co. Dublin Decree
Margaret Reilly	5 May 1848	£1.13.4	John Lavaria	Plaintiff	Co. Dublin Decree
Alexander Sinclair	5 May 1848	£8.11.8	Alicia Forde	Insolvent Court	Co. Dublin Decree
James Walsh	9 May 1848	£11.5.10	Charles Francis Atkinson	Insolvent Court	Co. Dublin Decree
Daniel Mulhern	10 May 1848	£6.1.10	Patrick Mulhern	Plaintiff	Co. Dublin Decree
Priscilla McLoughlin	11 May 1848	£6.8.8	Thomas Farrell	Insolvent Court	
Cornelius Shannon	15 May 1848	£16.8.4	Patrick Finan	Insolvent Court	City of Dublin Decree
John Farrell	18 May 1848	£36.0.0	Christina Coyle	Sub sheriff Co. Dublin	Queen's Bench Fiat
John Kilfoy	23 May 1848	£10.17.10	Joseph Younge	Insolvent Court	Co. Dublin Decree
John Rodger	23 May 1848	£14.8.5	Samuel Todd	Insolvent Court	St. Mary's Abbey Decree

Debtor name	Date committed	Amount	Plaintiff	Discharged By	Process of Committal
William Langton	30 May 1848	£3.9.3	John McCormick etc	Plaintiff Attorney	City of Dublin Decree
Owen Tho's Loyde	2 June 1848	£61.5.6	Stephen Pidgeon	Sub Sheriff	Exchequer Execution
Butler Creaghe	3 June 1848	£101.14.2	Thomas Dillon	Sub Sheriff	Exchequer Execution
Miles O'Neill	6 June 1848	£2.2.4	John Doran	Plaintiff	City of Dublin Decree
Arthur Faulkner	7 June 1848	£47.11.6	J.M. Hilles etc	Sheriff	Exchequer Execution
Patrick Brophy	10 June 1848	£3.19.3	John Doran	Plaintiff	City of Dublin Decree
Henry Newton	12 May 1848	£7.8.2	Michael Tracey	Plaintiff	Co. Dublin Decree
Same	12 May 1848	£6.17.1	William Reid	Insolvent Court	Co. Dublin Decree
Thomas Powell	12 May 1848	£10.2.0	Robert Gunn & John Corcoran	Insolvent Court	City of Dublin Decree

Debtor name	Date committed	Amount	Plaintiff	Discharged By	Process of Committal
Rachael Bingham	12 May 1848	£38.15.3	Patrick Fitzpatrick	Insolvent Court	Queen's Bench Decree
Hans Hartung	13 May 1848	£10.4.0	Martha Burge	Sub Sheriff	Exchequer Execution
Henry Newton	14 May 1848	£40.8.6	John Robertson	Insolvent Court	Exchequer Execution Detainer
Robert Davis	14 May 1848	£2.17.0	John Doran	Plaintiff	City of Dublin Decree
Catherine Dudley	21 May 1848	£3.11.1	Robt Nicholls Frizell	Plaintiff	Co. Dublin Decree
James Ashton	22 May 1848	£6.3.4	Wm Anderson	Plaintiff Attorney	Co. Dublin Decree
Humphrey Peare Jnr	22 May 1848	£91.12.11	Dundalk & Enniskillen Railway Co.	Plaintiff	Queen's Bench
Patrick Coughlan	22 May 1848	£72.0.0	William Hamilton Moffatt	Insolvent Court	Chancery Attachment
Owen Kelly	23 May 1848	£11.2.4	Augustine Flood	Plaintiff	City of Dublin Decree

Debtor name	Date committed	Amount	Plaintiff	Discharged By	Process of Committal
Simpson Gallagher	24 May 1848	£7.2.6	Sarah Jane Dee	Plaintiff	St. Mary's Abbey Decree
William Browne	26 May 1848	£50.6.6	Sir John Kennedy Bt	Plaintiff & Sub-sherriff	Exchequer Execution
John Mooney	27 May 1848	£1.19.3	William Dea Hare?	Plaintiff	City of Dublin Decree
Thomas Motherway	30 May 1848	£2.17.9	William Magee	Insolvent Court	Co. Dublin Decree
Robert Henry Hamill	5 July 1848	£40.5.9	Peter Doule	Sheriff	Exchequer Execution
Honoria Moran	6 July 1848	£20.0.0	Rev. N. Brindley Mahaffy	Sub Sheriff	Queen's Bench Exec'n
James Watt	8 July 1848	£212.14.5	Despard Taylor	Insolvent Court	Exchequer Execution
James Fitzgerald	10 July 1848	£2.13.11	Executors of Mary Ann Callan?	Insolvent Court	Co. Dublin Decree
William Jones	11 July 1848	£3.17.4	John Robinson	Insolvent Court	Co. Dublin Decree

Debtor name	Date committed	Amount	Plaintiff	Discharged By	Process of Committal
Edwin Stubbs	12 July 1848	£6.14.4	John Doran	Plaintiff	City of Dublin Decree
Hugh Thomas Stafford	14 July 1848	£83.16.8	James Wilcox	Sub Sheriff	Exchequer Execution
Peter Arthur King	22 July 1848	£16.16.7	Catherine Crawford	Insolvent Court	Queen's Bench
John Usher	22 July 1848	£4.6.11	Coleman Gardiner	Reported dead?	Co Galway Decree
Simon Martin	23 July 1848	£10.3.11	Thomas Bewley & William Hogg	Insolvent Court	Co. Dublin Decree
Same	22 July 1848	£10.3.11	same	Insolvent Court	Co. Dublin Decree
Patrick Daly	18 July 1848	£18.4.9	Thos Warren White et al	Insolvent Court	Common Pleas Exec'n
Xaverius Blake	28 July 1848	£14.17.6	Thomas Fulton	Insolvent Court	Queen's Bench Exec'n
James Gough	28 July 1848	£20.0.0	The Queen	N Kemmis Esq.	Forfeited Recognizance

Debtor name	Date committed	Amount	Plaintiff	Discharged By	Process of Committal
John Keating	31 July 1848	£3.3.3	Martin McKenny	Plaintiff	Co. Dublin Decree
Catherine Christian	2nd Aug 1848	£22.3.3	John Smith	Sub Sheriff	Exchequer Judge's Fiat
Patrick Kavanagh	4 Aug 1848	£15.7.4	William Kelly	Insolvent Court	City of Dublin Decree
Philip Daly	8 Aug 1848	£4.1.10	John Doran	Plaintiff	Co. Dublin Decree
James Toole	10 Aug 1848	£7.2.4	Sarah Harris	Petition discharged?	Co. Dublin Decree
Michael Kinsella	10 Aug 1848	£17.7.4	H. Stafford & Donnellan	Insolvent Court	Co. Dublin Decree
John Ryan	10 Aug 1848	£4.2.9	Patrick Rourke	Plaintiff Attorney	Co. Dublin Decree
James Sheridan	11 Aug 1848	£9.13.10	Maurice Connor		Co. Dublin Decree
Michael Connolly	18 Aug 1848	£2.10.4	Sylvester Moore	Plaintiff	Co. Dublin Decree
Deborah Rutland	21 Aug 1848	£1.2.4	Bernard Tier	Plaintiff Attorney	Co. Dublin Decree

Debtor name	Date committed	Amount	Plaintiff	Discharged By	Process of Committal
John McFarlane	23 Aug 1848	£11.7.10	H. S. Donnellan	Insolvent Court	Co. Dublin Decree
Edward McCann	24 Aug 1848	£8.7.7	Pat Fitzpatrick	Insolvent Court	Co. Dublin Decree
Henry S. Lincoln	25 Aug 1848	£45.1.1	John Joseph Nowlan	Insolvent Court	Exchequer Execution
Patrick Finnegan	26 Aug 1848	£2.7.0	Patrick Harrison	Insolvent Court	Malahide Decree
John L MacCartney	29 Aug 1848	£7.13.4	James Madden	Insolvent Court	City of Dublin Decree
Thomas Henry Williams	29 Aug 1848	£19.17.3	Thomas Walsh	Sub Sheriff	Co. Dublin Decree
Thomas Lawless	1 Sept 1848	£2.6.4	John Scully	Plaintiff Attorney	City of Dublin Decree
Benjamin Langson	1 Sept 1848	£7.15.0	Edward Browning	Insolvent Court	Chancery Attachment
Patrick Henry Lynch	2nd Sept 1848	£178.15.0	Martin Kerwin Blake	Sub Sheriff	Judges Fiat Common Pleas

Debtor name	Date committed	Amount	Plaintiff	Discharged By	Process of Committal
James John Campbell	6 Sept 1848	£10.8.6	Morris Myers	Insolvent Court	St. Mary's Abbey Decree
Patrick Connolly	7 Sept 1848	£37.10.10	John Conroy	Insolvent Court	Queen's Bench Exec'n
John L MacCartney	8 Sept 1848	£42.17.5	William Cairnes	Insolvent Court	Queen's Bench Exec'n
John Kighron	9 Sept 1848	£102.12.1	Wm Cash & Henry Ledgard	Insolvent Court	Common Pleas Exec'n
Patrick Healy	18 Sept 1848	£9.14.0	Thomas Butler	Plaintiff	Co Tipperary Decree
Edmond Cumming	18 Sept 1848	£2.2.3	Joseph Robt Commyns	Sheriff	City of Dublin Decree
George W. Bolton	25 Sept 1848	£10.11.4	Simon Boileau Golter?	Plaintiff Attorney	City of Dublin Decree
Edward Regan	27 Sept 1848	£87.7.11	Samuel Knox	Sheriff	Exchequer Execution
Mark A MacCartney	28 Sept 1848	£7.1.7	Rev. Pat Nagle	Insolvent Court	Co. Dublin Decree

Debtor name	Date committed	Amount	Plaintiff	Discharged By	Process of Committal
Robert Essex Burge	6 Oct 1848	£85.5.3	Dublin & Belfast Junction Railway Co.	Insolvent Court	Queen's Bench Exec'n
Richard Murray	10 Oct 1848	£7.9.4	Nathan & Nathaniel Dalton	Sub Sheriff	Co. Dublin Decree
Henry Kelly	10 Oct 1848	£0.6.5	Henry Elvidge	Plaintiff Attorney	City Decree Dismissal
George Fitzgerald	13 Oct 1848	£20.9.4	Patrick Purcell	Insolvent Court	Co. Dublin Decree
Thomas Biggs Lane	14 Oct 1848	£2.10.8	James Smith	Insolvent Court	Co Cork Decree
Paul King Bracken	16 Oct 1848	£61.18.11	Obadia P. Williams	Insolvent Court	Queen's Bench Exec'n
Jane Bridget O'Meara	21 Oct 1848	£92.1.3	Harloe Trumble Phibbs	Habeus Corpus of Four Courts	Queen's Bench Exec'n
Benjamin Williams	26 Oct 1848	£20.16.5	William Carey	Sub Sheriff	Exchequer Execution
Edward Johnston	28 Oct 1848	£3.5.10	Patrick Rooney	Sub Sheriff	Co. Dublin Decree

Debtor name	Date committed	Amount	Plaintiff	Discharged By	Process of Committal
James Lambert	4 Nov 1848	£14.0.10	Denis Farrell	Plaintiff	Co. Dublin Decree
Abraham Dowling	9 Nov 1848	£80.0.0	John Valentine Nixon	Sub Sheriff	Exchequer Judge's Fiat
Michael Clinton	10 Nov 1848	£10.18.4	Rev. Samuel Eccles	Insolvent Court	Co. Dublin Decree
James Fitzpatrick	10 Nov 1848	£32.10.0	Chris. & Eliz. Coughlan	Plaintiff	Exchequer Judge's Fiat
Patrick Foy	17 Nov 1848	£46.19.10	Charles Fitzgerald	Plaintiff	Exchequer Execution
Charles Marlton Gibbon Quantrille	24 Nov 1848	£31.9.6	Thomas Kearse	Sub Sheriff	Queen's Bench Exec'n
Henry Bunbury	6 Dec 1848	£129.5.3	John Parker	Insolvent Court	Queen's Bench Exec'n
Eliza Frances Beresford	7 Dec 1848	£33.5.0	John Samuel Hurst et al	Sub Sheriff	Exchequer Execution
Julia O'Connor	12 Dec 1848	£41.10.7	John Leake	Sheriff	Queen's Bench Exec'n

Debtor name	Date committed	Amount	Plaintiff	Discharged By	Process of Committal
Ismenia O'Connor	"	"	"	"	"
Julia O'Connor	12 Dec 1848	£77.19.2	Joseph L Camion	Sheriff	Exchequer Execution
Ismenia O'Connor	"	"	"	"	"
John Foster	9 Dec 1848	£20.0.0	The Queen	H. Kemmis Esq	Forfeited Recognizance
Benjamin Patterson	16 Dec 1848	£50.17.5	David Guthrie	Insolvent Court	Exchequer Execution
Taylor Read	16 Dec 1848	£59.5.10	John Summers D?	Plaintiff & Sherriff	Exchequer Execution
Clement Waters	1 Jan 1849	£20.9.4	Augustine Flood		Co. Dublin Decree
Peter Dalton	11 Jan 1849	£30.0.0	Clement Waters	Habeus Corpus	Queen's Bench Exec'n
Connell Dalton	11 Jan 1849	£30.0.0	Clement Waters	Habeus Corpus	Queen's Bench Exec'n
Peter Court Dalton	11 Jan 1849	£48.4.3	Executors of Walter Peter	Four Courts	Queen's Bench Exec'n

Debtor name	Date committed	Amount	Plaintiff	Discharged By	Process of Committal
John McCann	17 Jan 1849	£14.12.10	Bridget Gahan	Insolvent Court	Co. Dublin Decree
John Browne	23 Jan 1849	£37.16.0	Robert Shaw	Sheriff	Queen's Bench Judge's Fiat
William Carleton	23 Jan 1849	£61.7.0	William Bryan	Insolvent Court	Exchequer Execution
Patrick Dowdall	25 Jan 1849	£11.16.0	Hugh Maguire Esq.	Plaintiff	Co. Dublin Decree
Patrick Rickard	26 Jan 1849	£60.15.11	John Lynch	Insolvent Court	Exchequer Execution
John Farrell	27 Jan 1849	£12.9.1	Joseph Dodd	Insolvent Court	Co. Dublin Decree
John Sexton	12 Feb 1849	£136.0.0	Cornelius O'Brien	Insolvent Court	Queen's Bench Judge's Fiat
Mathew Gregan	15 Feb 1849	£105.7.3	Charlotte Mary Sweetman	Insolvent Court	Queen's Bench Exec'n
Jeremiah Tuthill	27 Feb 1849	£1249.7.8	John Percy	Sheriff	Common Pleas Exec'n

Debtor name	Date committed	Amount	Plaintiff	Discharged By	Process of Committal
Clement Ruskell	27 Feb 1849	£36.3.1	Manly Thacker	C. Warren Esq.	Common Pleas Exec'n
William West	1 Mar 1849	£138.5.11	William McHugh	Reported dead	Queen's Bench Exec'n
Mary Casey	2 Mar 1849	£7.8.8	Eleanor Casey	C. Warren Esq.	Chancery Attachment
John Hughes	30 Mar 1849	£34.18.9	William Thos D?	Insolvent Court	Chancery Attachment
Francis Edward Thomas	31 Mar 1849	£73.12.0	Charles Haskins	Sheriff	Queen's Bench Exec'n
Lewis Morris	22 Mar 1849	£27.1.11	Charles Palmer Archer	Habeus Corpus to Four Courts	Queen's Bench Exec'n
Andrew Mooney	26 Mar 1849	£61.17.3	James Hamilton	Insolvent Court	Queen's Bench Exec'n
Thomas Ormsby	5 April 1849	£245.10.1	James Walker Lyon	Sheriff	Queen's Bench Exec'n

Debtor name	Date committed	Amount	Plaintiff	Discharged By	Process of Committal
Christopher Kearns	10 April 1849	£19.18.9	Lawrence Malone	Four Courts Marshalsea	Exchequer Execution
Henry Bunbury	21 April 1849	£17.10.4	John Whitty	Insolvent Court	Co. Dublin Decree
Henry Eggleso	26 April 1849	£63.9.11	William Andrews	Insolvent Court	Exchequer Execution
Rosanna Meeley (widow)	27 April 1849	£30.8.4	William F. Bentley	Insolvent Court	City of Dublin Decree
Andrew Carty	1st May 1849	£53.12.9	Wm Coles	Sheriff	Chancery Attachment
Joseph Mooney	5 May 1849	£77.14.5	James Hickey	Sheriff	Queen's Bench Exec'n
John Willson	19 May 1849	£89.5.11	Charles Marsh	Insolvent Court	Exchequer Execution
Samuel P Lea	30 May 1849	£29.17.8	Lewis Harris	Sheriff	Exchequer Execution
James Jordan	25 Jan 1854	£13.3.5	James Murphy & Marcus Hughes	Insolvent Court	Co. Dublin Decree

Debtor name	Date committed	Amount	Plaintiff	Discharged By	Process of Committal
John Morrison	31st Jan 1854	£11.6.9	D Huffield Beatham	Insolvent Court	Co. Dublin Decree
Patrick Dowdall	6 Feb 1854	£15.0.10	James Lewis	Plaintiff & Sherriff	Co. Dublin Decree
Patrick A Fegan	7 Feb 1849	£13.15.10	Anna Eliza English	Insolvent Court	Co. Dublin Decree
Joseph Wallnutt	10 Feb 1954	£22.6.0	Thomas M. Nally	Plaintiff Attorney	Co. Dublin Decree
Francis Keely	10 Feb 1849	£22.6.0	same	same	Co. Dublin Decree
Edward Leeson	13 Feb 1854	£17.15.10	Sophia Bond	Insolvent Court	Co. Dublin Decree
Edward K. Holland	14 Feb 1849	£30.4.6	William Young & James Groves	Insolvent Court	Co. Dublin Decree
Cornelius O'Hare	16 Feb 1854	£26.4.10	Robert Allen Horden	Plaintiff Attorney	Co. Dublin Decree
John Hutton	18 Feb 1854	£74.6.7	Edward Dowling	Sheriff	Exchequer Execution
Same	20 Feb 1854	£30.3.8	James Barrett	Sheriff	Exchequer Execution
Same	20 Feb 1854	£58.3.10	Roberta Shepherd	Sheriff	Exchequer Execution

Debtor name	Date committed	Amount	Plaintiff	Discharged By	Process of Committal
Same	20 Feb 1854	£99.3.8	Richard Woodruffe	Sheriff	Common Pleas Exec'n
Same	20 Feb 1854	£14.19.2	Governor Bank of Ireland	Sheriff	Co. Dublin Decree
William Connolly	21 Feb 1854	£13.8.5	Thomas Bacon	Insolvent Court	Co. Dublin Decree
Henry Brady	23 Feb 1854	£20.9.10	Martin Bourke	Plaintiff Attorney	Co. Dublin Decree
Thomas Maguire	27 Feb 1854	£40.18.9	James B Kennedy & John Bell	Insolvent Court	Queen's Bench Exec'n
James D Scully	27 Feb 1854	£16.11.10	Fredk Robert Lees	Plaintiff Attorney	Co. Dublin Decree
John Hutton	28 Feb 1854	£139.3.6	Daniel Carrigan	Sheriff	Queen's Bench Exec'n
Same	28 Feb 1854	£79.17.0	John M Kenna	Sheriff	Exchequer Execution
Harvey P. L'Estrange	2nd Mar 1854	£305.12.7	John Jones	Insolvent Court	Common Pleas Court

Debtor name	Date committed	Amount	Plaintiff	Discharged By	Process of Committal
James S Gaskin	6 Mar 1854	£12.3.8	George Mulligan	Insolvent Court	Co. Dublin Decree
Thomas F. S Gunnley	9 Mar 1854	£34.19.11	Parker Molloy	Sheriff	Exchequer Execution
Joseph Brownrigg	11 Mar 1854	£38.4.7	James Oldham	Sheriff	Exchequer Execution
Patrick Brennan	16 Mar 1854	£8.11.8	J.J. Verschoyle Esq.	Plaintiff & Sherriff	Co. Dublin Decree
Butler Creagh	17 Mar 1854	£287.7.8	Maria Mahon	Sheriff	Exchequer Execution
Thomas Murphy	23 Mar 1854	£18.8.9	Joseph Watkins et al	Insolvent Court	Exchequer Execution
William N. Woods	25 Mar 1854	£37.18.1	Richard Tracey	Sheriff	Queen's Bench Exec'n
John Thomas Walker	13 June 1855	£40.9.6	Richard Woodruffe	Insolvent Court	Exchequer Execution
Edward Thorpe	15 June 1855	£55.11.5	James Birch Kennedy & John Bell	Insolvent Court	Co. Dublin Decree

Debtor name	Date committed	Amount	Plaintiff	Discharged By	Process of Committal
Pierce S. Butler	15 June 1855	£54.7.1	Charles Ammerman?	Insolvent Court	Queen's Bench Exec'n
Same	16 June 1855	£60.2.0	Sarah Buckmartin	Insolvent Court	Common Pleas Exec'n
Harry Cluff	25 June 1855	£5.8.9	Geo Thompson	Sheriff	Co. Dublin Decree
Jeremiah Loyne	15 July 1855	£43.1.8	Edward Darling	Insolvent Court	Common Pleas Exec'n
The Hon. Thomas Ffrench	25 July 1855	£1960.18.11	James Stirling	Insolvent Court	Queen's Bench Exec'n
Felix Boylan	27 July 1855	£39.13.8	James P. Madden	Insolvent Court	Common Pleas Court
John Stevenson	14 Aug 1855	£11.14.10	Thomas Dockrell	Insolvent Court	Co. Dublin Decree
Same	"	"	Thomas Johnston	"	Co Dublin Decree
Laurence R. Mooney	22 Aug 1855	£11.9.10	John Byrne	Sheriff	City of Dublin Decree

Debtor name	Date committed	Amount	Plaintiff	Discharged By	Process of Committal
Jacob Jackson Lunn	20 Aug 1855	£37.4.11	William Hutchinson et al	Insolvent Court	Common Pleas Court
Patrick Regan	17 Sep 1855	£32.2.10	Edward Gerd?	Insolvent Court	Common Pleas Court
Mathew Foot	2 Oct 1855	£39.11.0	Rt Hon Mervyn Viscount Powerscourt	Plaintiff Attorney	Co Wicklow Decree
Mary Eliz Butler	4 Oct 1855	£60.6.10	Stephen Pidgeon	Rt Hon Baron Greene	Judges Fiat
Gerald Connell	23 Oct 1855	£0.18.7	Patrick O'Brien	Paid by Deputy Gov.	Co. Dublin Decree
John Leverin	24 Oct 1855	£27.7.8	William Kenny	Plaintiff	Co. Dublin Decree
John Ford	26 Oct 1855	£13.15.10	Christopher Mooney	Insolvent Court	Co. Dublin Decree
Patrick Gormley	1 Nov 1855	£11.18.10	Findlater & Co.	Insolvent Court	Co. Dublin Decree
George Dickinson	5 Nov 1855	£8.15.10	James Downes	Deputy Governor	Co. Dublin Decree

Debtor name	Date committed	Amount	Plaintiff	Dis-charged By	Process of Committal
James Dowdall	31 Oct 1855	£40.2.1	Charles B Johnston	Sent to Four Courts Marshalsea	Exchequer Execution
Mathew Foot	12 Nov 1855	£43.8.1	Andrew Keogh	Sheriff	Queen's Bench Exec'n
Henry F Pilkington	13 Nov 1855	£14.16.3	Henry Bussell	Sheriff	Queen's Bench Exec'n
Geo S. Dickinson	24 Nov 1855	£5.5.8	Jane Parker	Paid by Governor	City of Dublin Decree
James Lube	24 Nov 1855	£19.10.5	Samuel Leader & William Leader	Insolvent Court	Common Pleas Exec'n
Owen Edward Lynch	27 Nov 1855	£14.8.0	Robert Gladstone	Insolvent Court	Exchequer Execution
Stephen Dowdall	30 Nov 1855	£15.0.8	Michael Larkin	Sheriff	Queen's Bench Exec'n
William A. Magrath	9 Jan 1860	£10.7.5	John S. Gormley	Insolvent Court	Co. Dublin Decree

Debtor name	Date committed	Amount	Plaintiff	Discharged By	Process of Committal
Thomas Gray	11 Jan 1860	£20.14.6	James Walsh	Plaintiff Attorney	Co. Dublin Decree
Richard D. Baker	24 Jan 1860	£28.19.5	Rev. James Paton	Insolvent Court	Common Pleas Exec'n
Thomas Mc Dermot	25 Jan 1860	£17.13.8	Robert Casey	Insolvent Court	City of Dublin Decree
Eliza Murphy	28 Jan 1860	£86.12.0	Peter McSweeney & George Delaney	Insolvent Court	Common Pleas Exec'n
William Crowthers	1 Feb 1860	£60.0.0	Edward Reilly	The Sheriff	Judges Fiat
Chas. P. Gavin	23 Feb 1860	£30.10.0	John Marshall	Plaintiff Attorney	Judges Execn.
Andrew Barr	5 Mar 1860	£32.14.0	Chas. Jas. Pownall	Insolvent Court	Exchequer Execution
Richard Croker	6 Mar 1860	£119.0.0	Robt. Grimshaw & Jas. Heron	Sheriff	Exchequer Execution
Same	9 Mar 1860	£12.19.10	Silas Ebenezer Weir	Sheriff	Co. Tyrone Execution

Debtor name	Date committed	Amount	Plaintiff	Discharged By	Process of Committal
Richard Langan	13 Mar 1860	£34.5.4	Thomas Carpenter	Paid the amount	Exchequer Execution
John Hunter	15 Mar 1860	£14.8.4	Joseph Smith Wilson	Paid Governor	Exchequer Execution
Martin Jos. Fitzsimon Kenny	21 Mar 1860	£175.0.0	Chas. Sears Lancaster	Sheriff	Judges Fiat
Capt. A.M. Robertson	17 Mar 1863	£208.7.1	Lewis Harris	Plaintiff & Sherriff	Co. Dublin Decree
Robt. Cooper	17 Mar 1863	£15.10.0	Peter Aungier?		Co. Dublin Decree
Capt. A.M. Robertson	17 Mar 1863	£210.18.3	Julius Calishoe	Writ of Habeus	Common Pleas Exec'n
Same	17 Mar 1863	£412.14.11	same	same	Queen's Bench Exec'n
Same	17 Mar 1863	£52.18.2	Henry Emanuel	Sheriff	Common Pleas Exec'n
John Wellington Browne	25 Mar 1863	£57.10.11	Thomas Perrier? Davis	Sheriff	Common Pleas Exec'n
James Duffy	27 Mar 1863	£41.11.5	Alex. Foy	Writ of Habeus	Exchequer Execution

Debtor name	Date committed	Amount	Plaintiff	Discharged By	Process of Committal
Arthur M. Robertson	28 Mar 1863	£13.18.1	Joseph Santry	Sheriff	Queen's Bench
Jane Brew	31 Mar 1863	£11.5.3	Jas. McDermott	Plaintiff Attorney	City of Dublin Decree
Robert Dillon	2 Apr. 1863	£11.5.3	?	Sheriff	Exchequer Execution
Edwd. Cavanagh	8 Apr 1863	£57.0.2	Fredk. Bidford et al		Exchequer Execution
Capt. A.M. Robertson	10 Apr. 1863	£74.15.11	John Freeman	Sheriff	Common Pleas Exec'n
Thos. F. Millington	10 Apr 1863	£14.12.2	Charlotte Kelly	Sheriff	Queen's Bench
A.M. Robertson	13 Apr 1863	£32.6.1	Elrington family	Sheriff	Common Pleas Exec'n
Richard B. Low	14 May 1867	£126.16.6	Joseph Sherry	Sheriff	Queen's Bench
Frederick Hitchcock	17 May 1867	£14.0.4	Charles Paslon?	Plaintiff Attorney	Co. Dublin Decree
Michael Kilroy	8 June 1867	£23.1.0			Exchequer Execution

Debtor name	Date committed	Amount	Plaintiff	Discharged By	Process of Committal
Fergus Farrell	10 June 1867	£52.3.3	Denis Scally	Plaintiff Attorney	Queen's Bench
John C. Clifford	12 June 1867	£34.4.11	Mary Pigott	Sheriff	Common Pleas Exec'n
Isaac Butt	12 June 1867	£59.17.8	Philip Fowells?	Paid Governor	Common Pleas Exec'n
same		£178.19.1	Thos. Darcy Johnston	Sheriff	Exchequer Execution
same		£20.16.4	James H. Kavanagh	Plaintiff Attorney	Co. Dublin Decree
same		£1985.17.10	Theophilus Bolton, Execr. of Charles Bolton Deceased.	Sheriff	Queen's Bench
same		£36.13.11	Edward Maunsell	Sheriff	Common Pleas Exec'n

Debtor name	Date committed	Amount	Plaintiff	Discharged By	Process of Committal
same		£564.5.11	Jas. Hewitt Sawyer & Richd. Sawyer for John Sawyer Decd.	Sheriff	Queen's Bench
same		£212.4.5	Charles Beaufort?	Sheriff	Exchequer Execution
same		£43.4.2	Edward Russell	Sheriff	Queen's Bench
same		£107.14.7	Chris. O'Brien	Sheriff	Queen's Bench
same		£48.17.0	Leon Smith & Will. Foster Grady	Sheriff	Exchequer Execution
same		£36.3.11	Brian Maunsell & George Augustus Elliott	Sheriff	Common Pleas Exec'n
same	14 Jun 1867	£57.8.3	James McDermott	Sheriff	City of Dublin Decree
same		£111.4.0	Robt. and John Peppard	Sheriff	Common Pleas Exec'n

Debtor name	Date committed	Amount	Plaintiff	Discharged By	Process of Committal
same		£318.15.0	Mathew John M. Coffey	Sheriff	Exchequer Execution
same		£36.12.2	Mary Pigott	Sheriff	Common Pleas Exec'n
same		£144.18.1	John Westin	Sheriff	Exchequer Execution
same		£67.19.3	Robert Grey	Sheriff	Exchequer Execution
same		£156.4.9	?	Sheriff	Exchequer Execution
same		£505.15.0	Thomas Wright	Sheriff	Exchequer Execution
same	15 Jun 1867	£116.2.1	John Tucker	Sheriff	Queen's Bench
same		£27.3.11	John Hancock	Sheriff	Queen's Bench
same		£20.19.1	David Stears	Paid Governor	Exchequer Execution
same		£96.16.10	Jonathan Richardson	Sheriff	Queen's Bench

Debtor name	Date committed	Amount	Plaintiff	Discharged By	Process of Committal
same		£1213.1.5	Thomas Smith Gore	Sheriff	Exchequer Execution
same	1 July 1867	£248.2.1	Pearse Rogers Nesbitt	Sheriff	Queen's Bench
same		£146.6.5	F. Stroker?	Sheriff	Exchequer Execution
same	6 July 1867	£140.6.11	F. Stroker?	Sheriff	Exchequer Execution
same	6 July 1867	£166.14.4	Marian?Gabriel	Sheriff	Common Pleas Exec'n
Richard B. Low	19 July 1867	£28.17.11	Gregory Kane	Sheriff	Common Pleas Exec'n
Richard Butler Low	19 July 1867	£120.10.9	Revd. Richard Church Stackpoole	Sheriff	Exchequer Execution
John Blunden	20 July 1867	£123.1.11	Arthur Gardiner	Sheriff	Exchequer Execution
John Neill	25 July 1867	£11.1.0	Mary Ann Murphy	Insolvent Court	Co. Dublin Decree
Isaac Butt	30 July 1867	£551.12.1	Henrietta V. Jackson	Sheriff	Queen's Bench

Debtor name	Date committed	Amount	Plaintiff	Discharged By	Process of Committal
Richard B. Low	2 Aug 1867	£17.18.2	Pigot family	Sheriff	Queen's Bench

SOURCES

(A)PRIMARY

GENERAL REGISTER OFFICE, DUBLIN, ABBEY STREET, DUBLIN
Selected registrations of births, marriages and deaths.

NATIONAL ARCHIVES , BISHOP STREET, DUBLIN
Chief Secretary's Office, Convict Department, Transportation Registers: GPO TR 1-15,1837-57 , or MFS 56/1-5.
Chief Secretary's Office, Convict Department, prisoners' petitions and cases: MFS 57/1-14.
Convict Department, convict reference files: MFS 59/1-77
Convict Department, Free Settlers' Papers, 1828-52:MFS 59/76 &
MFS 60/1-3.
Convict Reference Books 1836-1922, CON CRB 1-16.
Court Service, Petty Sessions Order Books, (MFGS/58/1–3432.)
Tralee, MFGS 58/ 2772-4
Trim, MFGS 58/2820.
General Prison's Board penal files, 1877-1926 (draft) , GPB/PEN.
Philipstown Prison register of convicts, GPO/ PN 3. 1849-62.
Philipstown Convict Character Book. GPO/PN 5. 1849-1862.
Prison Registers: MFGS 51/ 1-163.
Prison Letters and Correspondence. 1850-1924. Available on the open shelves.
State Papers, Register of Convicts on Convict Ships, 1851-53, MFS 60/3.
South Dublin Union Register of Admissions 1851. MFGS 52/031.

REGISTRY OF DEEDS , KING'S INN, HENRIETTA STREET, DUBLIN

1845- 20- 83.
1845-6-240. Irwin to Percival.
1853- 23-101.
1857-16 -130. McGetrick to McGetrick.

PRINTED

Barrow, John Henry, Ed., *The Mirror of Parliament. Debates, Proceedings Etc. of the Imperial Parliament of Great Britain and Ireland, 1837-8,* Volume 1.
Dublin University Magazine, 'Irish Convict Prisons', Feb. 1858. Pages 166-72.
Irish Quarterly Review 'Appendix to Records, Irish Convict Prisons', vol. viii, Jan 1859, p. i- xxiii .
Irish Universities Nutrition Alliance. North/South Ireland Food Consumption Survey. Summary Report. 2001
Matheson, Sir Robert E., *A Special Report on the Surnames of Ireland with notes as to Numerical strength etc.* Alex Thom & Co., Dublin. 1909.
O'Donovan, John, Editor, *Annals of the Kingdom of Ireland by the Four Masters*, 7 volumes, Hodges and Smith, Grafton Street Dublin, 1851.
Reid,Thomas, *Travels in Ireland in the Year 1822,* Longman, Hurst, Rees, Orme, and Brown, 1823.

INTERNET

Ancestry. http://www.ancestry.co.uk/ . Census of England 1841, 1851,1861
*Gale,19th Century British Library Newspapers, Part 1,*http://find.galegroup.com.
    Freeman's Journal, Jan 01, 1820 - Sep 29, 1900.
—— *The Pall Mall Gazette* (London, England), 'The Wren of the Curragh'. No. 1- 4, October 15-19 1867,

Google Books. http:// books.google.com/ Long, George. *Penny Cyclopaedia of the Society for the Diffusion of Useful Knowledge*, Volumes 13-14. C Knight 1839. London ,Charles Knight and Co.

――――Forty-fifth report of the Inspector-generals of prisons in Ireland for 1866. 1867. X

National Archives of Ireland. http://www.nationalarchives.ie.Ireland-Australia transportation database

――――Census of Ireland 1901, http://www.census.nationalarchives.ie.

National Archives. http://www.nationalarchives.gov.uk/

Origins. http://www.origins.net. *Irish Origins Census of Elphin 1749,*

――――*Griffith's Valuation,* 1848-1864

Ordnance Survey of Ireland. http://www.osi.ie .

Proquest Information and Learning Company. House of Commons Parliamentary Papers Online. http://parlipapers.chadwyck.co.uk.

1809 (265) (Ireland.) Report from the commissioners appointed to inquire into and inspect the condition and government of the state prisons and other gaols in Ireland.

―――― Inspector of Prisons annual reports 1820-1878.

――――(194)Convicts(Ireland).Return of the names of convicts discharged from the several gaols in Ireland, before the expiration of their sentences, since 1st May 1835, &c.

――――Corporations Ireland. Vol. 24 , 1836.

――――1839 (486) Report from the Select Committee of the House of Lords, appointed to enquire into the state of Ireland in respect of crime.

――――1845 (296) Spirits. Spirits (Ireland). Accounts relative to foreign and British spirits, from the year 1780 to 1844 inclusive

――――1856 [2087-I] [2087-II] The census of Ireland for the year 1851. Part V. Tables of deaths. Vol. II.

―――― 1856 [2068] Second annual report of the directors of convict prisons in Ireland, for the year ended 31st December, 1855.

――――The census of Ireland for the year 1861. Part IV. Report and tables relating to the religious professions, education, and occupations of the people. Vol. II.

―――― 1862 (377) Alice Delin. Copies of the depositions taken at a coroner's inquest held at Tullamore.

――――19th Century House of Commons Sessional Papers, Vol. 11 page 353. February 15, 1864.

———1866 (147). Copy of the report of the inspectors general of prisons in Ireland to his Excellency the Lord Lieutenant with regard to the escape of James Stephens.

—— Reports of the General Prison Board 1879-1890.

—— 1882 [C.3268] Census of Ireland, 1881. Part I. Vol. IV. Province of Connaught.

NEWSPAPERS AND PERIODICALS

Irish Builder, Vol. XVI, no. 348, page 175, June 15, 1874. 'Newgate Prison, Green St. Dublin'.

*Irish Builde*r, Vol. XVIII, February 1875. 'County Courthouses and County Gaols in Ireland'.

Irish Times, 1859-2007, via ProQuest Historical Newspapers website.

Irish Times . January 17, 2011.

The British Medical Journal, March 11, 1882.

(B)SECONDARY

REFERENCE

Begley, Donal F., editor, *Irish Genealogy - a Record Finder* , Heraldic Arts Ltd., Trinity Street, Dublin 2. 1981.

Grenham, John. *Tracing Your Irish Ancestors: the Complete Guide*. Third Edition.Gill& Macmillan, 2006.

Hanks, Patrick and Hodges, Flavia. *Dictionary of Surnames.* Oxford Univ. Press, 1996.

Hayes,Richard J. Ed. *Manuscript sources for the History of Irish Civilisation.* 11 volumes. Boston 1965. Supplement. 1965-75. 3 volumes. Boston 1979.

Lewis, Samuel , *A Topigraphical Dictionary of Ireland.* London 1837.

MacLysaght, Edward. *Surnames of Ireland.* Irish Academic Press Ltd. 1991.

—— *Supplement to Irish Families.* Helicon Ltd. 1964.

——*More Irish Families.* O'Gorman Ltd. 1960.

O'Laughlin, Michael C. *Families of County Kerry*, Ireland. Irish Genealogical Foundation, Kansas Missouri 1994.

GENERAL

Ahern, Michael. *Clonmel County Gaol.* 2010.

Carey, Tim. Mountjoy. *The Story of a Prison.* Collins press. 2000.

Conlon, Michael V. 'Debtors in Cork Gaols, 1705-1872'. *Journal of the Cork Historical & Archaeological Society*, No. 47 1942, pages 9-23.

Connolly, Philomena, 'The Medieval Irish Plea Rolls: an Introduction', *Irish Archives*, Spring 1995, pages 3-11.

Costello, Con. *A Most Delightful Station.* Collins Press 1996.

Curtin, Geraldine. 'Female Prisoners in Galway Gaol in the Late Nineteenth Century'. *Journal of the Galway Archaeological and Historical Society.* Vol. 54, (2002), pages 175 -182.

Dempsey, M., Geary, R.C. *Irish Itinerants- some demographic, economic and educational aspects.* Economic and Social Research Institute. 1979.

Finnane, Mark. *Insanity and the insane in post-famine Ireland.* Taylor and Francis, 1981.

Geoghegan, Patrick M. *Liberator. The life and Death of Daniel O'Connell 1830-1847.* Gill
and Macmillian. 2010.

Gmelch, Sharon. *Tinkers and Travellers.* O'Brien Press. Dublin 1975.

Heaney, H.J. 'Ireland's First Prison Library'. *Library History.* No. 3, pages 59-62, Autumn   1973.

——'Ireland's Penitentiary 1820-31: an experiment that failed'. *Studia Hibernica*, No. 14. 1974, pages 28-39.

Hirschel, David, Hirschel, J. David, Wakefiled, William O., Sasse, Scott, *Criminal Justice in England and the United States* . Jones & Bartlett Learning, 2007.

Kelly, Tim. 'Ennis County Jail'. *North Munster Antiquarian Journal* 16,1973-4,pages 66-69.

Komlos, John editor, *Stature, Living Standards, and Economic Development: Essays in Anthro-pometric History.* 'The Heights of the British and the Irish c. 1800-1815: Evidence from Recruits to the East India Company's Army', pages 39-59, Cormac Ó Gráda. University of Chicago Press, 1994.

Lawlor, Rebecca Sharon, *Crime in nineteenth-century Ireland: Grangegorman female penitentiary and Richmond male penitentiary, with reference to juveniles and women, 1836-60.* Thesis. NUI Maynooth, Mar 2012.

Leigh, Samuel, *Leigh's New Picture of London.* Leigh and Co. 1839,via Google Books, http://books.google.com.

McConnon,Mary, 'The Kilmainham Gaol Registers 1798 to 1823: List of Convicts from County Louth'. *Journal of the County Louth Archaeological and Historical Society,* Vol. 23, No. 4(1996) pages 413-447. Via *JStor* website.

McGowan, James ' Nineteenth Century Developments in Irish Prison Administration'. *Administration.* No 26. 1978, pages 496-508. Via *Jstor* website.

Mitchell, James, ' The Prisons of Galway: Background to the Inspector General's Reports, 1796-1818'. *Journal of the Galway Archaeological and Historical Society,* Vol. 49 (1997), pages 1-21. Via *JStor* website.

Mitchel, John , *Jail Journal, Or, Five Years in British Prisons,* M.H. Gill & Son, 1854.

Mokyr, Joel and O'Grada, Cormac. 'The Height of Irishmen and Englishmen in the 1770s:Some Evidence from the East India Company Army Records', *Eighteenth-Century Ireland / Iris an dá chultúr,* Vol. 4 (1989), pages 83-92.

Murphy, Sean J. 'A Survey of Irish Surnames 1992-97 (Draft)', pages 14-27, *Studies in Irish Genealogy and Heraldry*, Windgates,County Wicklow, 2009, published online at http://homepage.eircom.net/~seanjmurphy/studies/surnames.pdf.

—— http://homepage.eircom.net/~seanjmurphy/nai/courts.html

——*A Guide to the National Archives of Ireland,* \http://homepage.eircom.net/~seanjmurphy/nai/

National Library of Ireland. *An Index of Surnames of Householders in Griffith's Valuation and Tithe Applotment Books Co. Mayo.* NLI 1964.

New Jersey Law Revison Commission. http://www.lawrev.state.nj.us,'Relating to Civil Arrest Capias ad Respondendum et Satisfaciendum'. Final Report, 1997 page 1-5.

Nowlan, A.J. 'Kilmainham Gaol'. *Dublin Historical Record.* No. 15.1960, pages 105-115.

O'Brien, Joseph B. *Dear Dirty Dublin: A City in Distress 1899-1916.* 1982.

O'Connor, Patrick. 'Debtors in Dublin Prisons'. *Dublin Historical Record* Vol. 6, No. 2 (Mar.- May, 1944), pages 75-80; Vol. 7, No.1(Dec. 1944- Feb. 1945) pages 34-38.

O'Grada, Cormac , 'Heights in Tipperary in the 1840s : evidence from prison registers', *Irish Economic and Social History,* 18 : 24-33, Manchester University Press, 1991. Via Research_Online@UCD.

———— *Ireland: A New Economic History,* 1780-1939. 1994.

O'Sullivan, John L. *Cork City Gaol.* Ballyheada Press. 1996.

O'Sullivan, Niamh. *Every Dark Hour. A History of Kilmainham Jail.* Liberties Press. 2007.

Rottman, David B. *The Population Structure and Living Circumstances of Irish Travellers : results from 1981 census of Traveller families.* ESRI. Paper No. 131, July 1986.

Shuinéar, Sinead Ni, 'Apocrypha to Canon: Inventing Irish Traveller History' . *History Ireland* , Vol. 12, no. 4, Winter 2004. Pages 15-19.

Slevin, Fiona, By hereditary virtues - a history of Lough Rynn. Coolabawn Publishing, 2006.

Smith, Beverly A. 'The Female Prisoner of Ireland 1855-1878', *Federal Probation,*Vol. 54, Issue 4(Dec 1990), pages 69-81.

———— 'Irish Prison Doctors - Men in the Middle, 1865-90. *Medical History*, 1982, 26: pages 371-394.

———— 'Ireland's Ennis Inebriates' Reformatory: A 19th Century Example of Failed Institutional Reform'. *Fed. Probation* 53 (1989). Pages 53-64.

Warburton, James , Whitelaw, James, Walsh, Robert, *History of the City of Dublin*, Volume 2,T. Cadell and W. Davies, London, 1818. Googlebooks.

Whelan, Bernadette (ed.) W*omen and Paid Work in Ireland, 1500-1930* . Lohan, Rena .'Matrons in Mountjoy Female Convict Prison, 1858-83', pages 86-101.
Four Courts Press 2000.

White, Terence De Vere, *The Road to Excess*, Browne and Nolan, 1946.

INTERNET

Ancestry, www.ancestry.co.uk.

Byrne,Michael.*HistoryofTullamoreGaol* www.offalyhistory.com/articles/88/1/ . Published 9/1/2007.

Cork City Jail Heritage Centre, http://corkcitygaol.com/about/history/

Familysearch, http://www.familysearch.org/eng/library

——https://wiki.familysearch.org/en/Ireland_Court_Records

Findmypast.ie

Grangegorman Community Museum, *http://www.grangegorman.ie.*

Grenham, John. www.johngrenham.com/.../ occupational%20%20 records.doc

Archiseek, http://ireland.archiseek.com

www.historyeye.ie

Irish Family History Foundation, http://www.rootsireland.ie/

Irish History Online. http://www.irishhistoryonline.ie/

JStor. http://www.jstor.org

The law Reform Commission, Report LRC 27, 1988, http://www.lawreform.ie/_fileupload/Reports/rDebtCollection1.pdf

Lyons, Jane, http://myhome.ispdr.net.au/~mgrogan/cork/jane_prison.htm. 1999.

Co. Kildare Online Electronic History Journal, http://www.kildare.ie/library/ehistory.

Mitchell,Jim,http://www.allbusiness.com/public-administration/justice-public-order/.December 1 2003.

Murphy, Sean J, *Centre for Irish Genealogical and Historical Studies ,* 1998-2010, http://homepage.eircom.net/~seanjmurphy/

National Archives, www.nationalarchives.gov.uk/records/research-guides/ bankrupts-insolvent-1710-1869.htm.

Origins, www.origins.net.

Sligo Jail. http://www.sligotown.net/sligogaol.shtml

Traveller surnames by locality, 1953 Schools Questionnaire. www.travellerheritage.ie/1953_names_by_locality.asp.

INDEX

Agrarian unrest, *xiv*,37,64

Aliases, (problem of),11,28,55,75-6,82

Athy Jail,*xi*,53-8,84,107,114,115

Bridewells,*viii,xi,xiv,*24,25,53,62,67, 79,113,114

Carrick Jail, 82,84,107,114

Castlebar Jail, 3-12,28,36,71,114

Clonmel Jail,34,64-7,78,80,85,114,115

Convicts,*vii,viii,x-xiv,*21,32-4,39,48, 51,52,59-61,70,72-4,76,81,114,115

Cork City Jail, 39-40,57,86

Cork County Jail,28,37-9,43,45,64,86- 90,108

Crofton System, *viii,xi,*61,76

County Jails,*viii,x,x*i,16,28,35,36,42, 43,44,45,62,65,67,78,79,80,81

Cruelty to animals (crime), 82

Curragh "Wrens", 55-8,79

Debtors,*xi*,28,29,30,31,33,34,38,39,40, 41-7,48,67,79,81,115,116-154

Drunkards, 2,22,23,26,35,40,48,115

Dublin,*xv*,1,2,21-4,27,32-5,41-5,48-9, 51,55,56,60,62,63,69,71,73,76,77,80, 81,82

Dundrum Central Mental Hospi- tal,63,72

Ennis Inebriate Reformatory,18- 20,90,108,114,115

Excise Offenders, 13-16,70,81,115

Faction Fighting, 78,81

Famine, the Great, *x*,1,14,24,29, 34,35, 38,48,78,79

Felons, 1,33,48,49,81

Firearm regulation breaches,83

Fry, Elizabeth,*x*,21

Galway,*x,xiv*,6,11,37,50,56,71,91

General Prisons Board, *vii,xii,xiv*,24, 36, 68, 71,73,74,80

Grangegorman Lane Women's Prison, *vii,ix,x,xi,xii*,21-6,35,51,63,75,92, 94,108-9,114,115

House of Correction institutions, 1,37

Howard, John, *x*

Inspector of Prisons Reports,*x,xiii*, 1,16,22,27,32,35,45,52,53,56,57,68, 69,70,7181

Juvenile Offenders, *viii,xi*,1,60, 61, 67, 75,115

Kilmainham Jail, *x,xii,xiv*,3,17,32-36,42-46,49,81-2,94,114,115,116-154

Limerick Jail, 37,42,43,46,96,110,115

Longford Jail, 11,97,115

Lunatics, *xi*,24,25,62-3,81

Marques, Dominic(Governor Grangegorman and Richmond Bridewell), 1,22

Matheson, Sir Robert, 8,31

Military Prisoners, 2,33,40,49,66,115

Mountjoy Jail,Dublin,*xi*,51-2,59,60,61,81,98,110,111,114,115

Naas Jail, 36,53-58,79,99,114,115

Nenagh Jail,xiv,42,43,46,64,67, 100,115

Newgate Jail, Dublin,*vii,x,xi*,1,48-50, 51, 61,71,100,114

O'Connell, Daniel, 1

Philipstown Jail, *xi,xiv*,52,59-61,76, 82, 101,114,115

Prison Correspondence, 71-3

Queen's County Jail (Portlaoise) *xi*,78,83,114

Railway Crime,81,82

Rawlins, Marian (matron of Grangegorman), 21

Rescue (crime),66,78

Richmond Lunatic Asylum, 24,25,62,63,115

Richmond Bridewell, *vii,x,xii*,1-2,22,23,51,69,75,101,110,114,115

Richmond Penitentiary, *ix*,21

Rioting, 65,66,78

Sacrilege (crime), 60,82

164

Sligo Jail, 3,11,12,13-17, 42,43, 45,46, 47,70.79,81,111,114,115

Stephens, James (Fenian escapee),1

Tralee Jail, *x*,3,27-31,45,104,111,114

Travellers, 3-12

Vagrancy/Vagrants,*xi*,22,23,35,37, 43,48, 66,69,78,81,115

Viceroy (Lord Lieutenant) Pardons, 60,70

Lightning Source UK Ltd.
Milton Keynes UK
UKOW06f0913221113

221624UK00008B/337/P